The Prison Sermons

by Rick Davis

ζηναν

Zenas Publishing House
P.O. Box 1206
Bryan, Texas 77806

xulon PRESS

Table of Contents

—⁓—

Acknowledgments

—〜〜—

I thank Jesus Christ, my Lord and my God, for giving me this little work to do, "for it is God who works in you to will and to act according to his good purpose" (Phil. 2:13). To Him belongs all glory. May He bless this little book abundantly, and may it serve as living water flowing into the hearts of many.

I thank my wife, Carolyn, for her steadfast commitment and support, and especially for her patience with my time away to go into prisons. Caring for our six children during my absences when I go into prison is a burden, one that I am thankful she willingly bears.

I am grateful for the help and encouragement of many beloved friends, all of whom I cannot possibly list. They include Pat Howard, Dub Pearson, Travis Bryan III, David Barron, David Toups, Lane and Beth Ann Thibodeaux, Steve Elmendorf, Matt Prochaska and his father Ernie (who is also one of my fathers in the faith), Tom Rodgers, Al Bradley, Laurie Calvin, Misty Cook, Harry Coyle (another of my fathers in the faith) and pastor Evan Henderson.

I thank my beloved staff: Bob Odstrcil ("Bob the bailiff"), Evonne Taylor (my secretary), Kristie Evans (my court coordinator), and Carolyn White (my court reporter). I often tell the lawyers that my job as a judge is easy. I simply go where

Kristie and Evonne tell me to go, and I say what Carolyn White says that I said. They put up with my many shortcomings day in and day out, and they share my joy and anguish.

There are four ministries that have helped me greatly over the years and which I wish to acknowledge. First, as will become evident in the pages that follow, *Campus Crusade for Christ* played an important part in my conversion, and the teachings I heard from Dr. Howard Hendricks at KC83, a Campus Crusade Christmas conference, set me on a mission.

Second, for nearly two decades, I have been greatly blessed by and am thankful for the work of Dr. Dave Reagan and the folks at Lamb & Lion Ministries. Through them, God has given me a keen interest in the soon return of the Lord Jesus. Further, in addition to internet research, old copies of the *Lamplighter* magazine were a valuable source of factual information for the chapter on the Signs of the Times and the Day of the Lord.

Third, Bible Study Fellowship (BSF) has enriched the lives of a multitude of men and women over the past several decades, me included. I have benefited from BSF's ministry for more than seven years, and I am grateful to the men and women in BSF leadership. I am thankful for the investment of their time, efforts and prayers into the lives of myself and a multitude of others. While I could not possibly name all who have blessed me through their labors, Lee Askins, Steve Gustitis, Kyle Davis, Dick Davison, Warren Reed, Bob Howard, Ryan Womack, Jack Shell, Bob Nordhaus and Bob Bilberry are or were in leadership since I have been a member, and I count them all among my blessings.

Fourth, in December 2001, while my wife and I were teaching their daughter's fifth grade Sunday school class, Bill and Jan Coates gave us a copy of the message *Hell's Best Kept Secret* by Ray Comfort. This message and others by Ray Comfort have greatly helped me to understand the biblical approach to evangelism and the proper function of God's law in making us aware of our need for a Savior. For that teaching, I am also grateful. It inspires me to be like the man on George Street.[1]

Finally, Charles Haddon Spurgeon (1832-1892), that prince of preachers from England, once wrote:

> The man who never reads will never be read; he who never quotes will never be quoted. He who will not use the thoughts of other men's brains, proves that he has no brains of his own. Brethren, what is true of ministers is true of all our people. YOU need to read. Renounce as much as you will all light literature, but study as much as possible sound theological works, especially the Puritanic writers, and expositions of the Bible.[2]

To that end, I read a lot, and I sometimes quote those whom I read. In this little book, I have earnestly endeavored to attribute all quotes properly. If I have erred in that regard, I humbly hope that charitable readers know that the errors were unintentional and that they will gently point them out to me that the errors might be corrected in any possible future revision.

CHAPTER 1

Introduction

—ᴍ—

I. The Crucible of Human Suffering

Having served as a district judge in the state of Texas for over six years, I have sent many men and women to prison. I have told many of them at sentencing that I take no pleasure in doing it. Indeed, I often mourn inwardly at the suffering that I see day in and day out.

Courtrooms are crucibles of human suffering. Very few joyful things happen in a courtroom, and the suffering there often affects many more lives than those of the defendants on trial. The very fact that someone is in court means that he is alleged either to have committed a crime, to have breached his contract, to have failed to look out for his neighbor (thereby injuring him), or to have failed at marriage. Were it not for the sinfulness of man, we would not need courtrooms. We are all, by nature, inherently selfish and rebellious against God.

II. A Message of Hope

My bailiff, Bob Odstrcil, is a long time friend of a dear lady named Pat Howard who was his high school classmate.

She is involved in a prison ministry called The Association of Ex-Offenders (TAX), and has been for over fifteen years. Bob introduced her to me about three years ago.

Pat asked me if I wanted to come to a prison unit in Huntsville, Texas to serve as a guest speaker to a group of inmates. She and I got to know each other when I accepted the invitation and went back several times. Though she is a generation older than I, she and I have become good friends. We are siblings in the faith, you could say, because we share the same Lord, Jesus Christ. Pat Howard has had many struggles and many trials in her life. Some of her hardships have been profoundly difficult, but there is no bitterness about her.

For many years, Pat has served as "broken bread and poured out wine" for many inmates. Quite a few love her like a mother. Indeed, some of the inmates in prison have never had a mother to speak of. On more than one occasion, I have seen her lead a group of inmates in singing "Happy Birthday" to another inmate who has never had anyone sing it to him in his entire life. Some of these inmates have never received a birthday card (let alone a birthday gift) in their entire lives.

I am very grateful to Pat for introducing me to prison ministry. Pat and others involved in TAX have told me that I bless the men greatly when I come out to speak to them, but I think that I must reap the greater blessing. I have earnestly enjoyed doing this sort of ministry work. It is a true joy.

The first time that I went into a prison to preach was August 3, 2004 at a meeting of the TAX chapter at the Estelle Unit in Huntsville, Texas. I was a little apprehensive at first. I was concerned that I might come across a man whom I had sent to prison, and I expected that I would encounter substantial resentment.

What I found instead were some of the most genuine, most caring, most loving Christians that I have ever encountered. I saw first hand how God had taken these broken men and turned them into something amazing: men who loved the Lord passionately.

I remember one inmate named Patrick who gave his testimony at the beginning of that first meeting. He was truly a changed man. He told us of his military service in Vietnam, of losing his best friend to a sniper, and of his own actions in that war that he longed to forget. He had a hard time telling us about these things. It hurt for him to tell the story. He spoke of his long downward spiral into a life of drugs and other crimes. Then, he told us how Jesus Christ had made him a new man.

He also enjoyed the message I gave that night. At the end of the meeting, he said exuberantly, "I feel so clean!" Oh, what an unspeakably great privilege it is to teach men that they truly can be cleaned by God, completely separated in God's sight from their former deeds! God so loved each one of them that he gave his one and only Son that whoever of them believes shall not perish but have eternal life (John 3:16).

Another inmate came up to me at the end of that first meeting. He shook my hand heartily and thanked me for coming. He said, "I would have loved to have been sentenced by a judge like you!" I chuckled inwardly, "God bless that man!" Truly, I am not worthy of the kindness, honor, and affection that some of these inmates have shown me.

Another good friend of mine, Dub Pearson, took me out to speak at the TAX Chapter of the Pack Unit in Navasota, Texas. I found the same hunger for the Word and genuineness in the inmates there that I had seen at the Estelle Unit. Dub and I enjoyed good fellowship on the way home. As we were discussing the evening and how attentive the men were, Dub said, "When you preach to these men, they often nod their heads in agreement and say to themselves, 'He's talking to me.' When you preach to people in the free world, they often sit in their pews, nudge their neighbor and say, 'He's talking to you.'" He is so right. There is no pride among these men. Their candor and honesty are so refreshing.

III. Felons at Heart

As you read the ensuing chapters, you will see that one of my favorite quotes is from the June 1st reading of the Oswald Chambers' devotional *My Utmost for His Highest*:

> When God wants to show you what human nature is like apart from Himself, He has to show it you in yourself. If the Spirit of God has given you a vision of what you are apart from the grace of God (and He only does it when His Spirit is at work), you know there is no criminal who is half so bad in actuality as you know yourself to be in possibility.[3]

That quote is so true. One reason that I enjoy this work so much is that I can identify with the inmates. I reflect on my own life, my own rebelliousness against God, and the many forks in my own road. I know in my heart of hearts that, but for the grace of God, I could be right there among them.

We are all felons at heart. Some of us have never acted on our evil, felonious thoughts. Others of us have, but simply have not been caught. If you are a reader in the free world, does this statement offend you? If it does, your very soul may be in danger of damnation.

Have you ever told a lie, even just once? Have you ever stolen anything (value is insignificant)? Have you ever committed adultery? If you have not, have you ever lusted for another not your spouse? If so, then you have committed adultery in God's sight. Have you ever had a hateful thought towards another? Then, you are guilty of murder. In our society, we have numbed ourselves to the fact that God sees our thought lives. When we judge ourselves in the light of

God's law, we are all lying, thieving, adulterous murderers at heart (and worse!).

With this understanding of the darkness of my own heart, I know that I could have been a murderer, an adulterer, a swindler, a drug dealer, or a fraud. I could have been an embezzler, a pimp, a pornographer, a whoremonger, a forger, or a racist. I could have been any of these things or worse. This admission is not false modesty. Instead, what I am saying about myself is entirely biblical. In Jeremiah 17:9, it is written, "The heart is deceitful above all things and beyond cure. Who can understand it?"

Knowing that God sees my thought life makes me fear God all the more. "I the LORD search the heart and examine the mind, to reward a man according to his conduct, according to what his deeds deserve" (Jer. 17:10). Knowing how bad my heart is apart from the redeeming grace of God makes it quite easy for me to want to reach inmates in prison with the life changing gospel of Jesus Christ.

IV. The Parentless Children

In fact, I truly care about these poor people. Many of the defendants who come before me have no fathers. Many do not know their mothers, either. I presided over a juvenile delinquency proceeding recently[4] involving a young man whose mother was sent to prison when he was a toddler. His father is unknown. It is not uncommon to find an inmate whose mother or father (and sometimes both) were in prison when he was growing up.

In May 2005, I sent a repeat offender and drug dealer to prison for forty years. I remember that he seemed proud of the fact that he had gotten three different women pregnant at the same time prior to his incarceration.

In August 2006, I sent a man to prison for life for raping a seven-year-old girl. The man's pre-sentence investigation report indicated that he had a history of nine felony arrests (at least four of which resulted in convictions) and eleven misdemeanor arrests (at least eight of which resulted in conviction). The psychologist's assessment of the sexual preference of that man revealed that he had molested at least four other children over his lifetime, slept with prostitutes on at least eight occasions, had affairs with fifteen women besides one of his wives, and on three occasions had sex with strangers. The report also stated "The defendant commented that he has other children with other women, but he regretted that he was unable to remember any of their names and admitted that some of the children he has never met."

In that same month, I signed an order for protective custody in a Child Protective Services case allowing the authorities to pick up the children of a woman who had five children from four different men. That is not counting two other children born of this woman who were already in the custody of their own two different fathers.

Who is raising this multitude of children who are the product of totally irresponsible men and women? No one is. And this statement is not limited to kids born in poor households. Many children of affluent parents have mothers and fathers bound by chains of their own making because they have yielded to the lust of the eyes, the lust of the flesh, and the pride of life. I know of families living in ten thousand square foot, plushy carpeted, air conditioned personal prisons with well manicured lawns. These absent parents, trying to assuage their own guilt, give their children all the pleasures this world has to offer. These latter children are nearly just as fatherless as the former. And, thus, many inmates come from families that you would least likely expect.

Eighteenth-century Brethren writer J.B. Stoney wrote, "It is a good sign when children prefer their home to any other place. How blessed if this were true of each of us with respect to our Father's house. The reason of our not doing so is that we do not sufficiently know the joy of it." If this statement is true, how much more true is it of the multitude of children who have no earthly father to provide at least a poor, weak example of our heavenly Father's love for us!

These parentless children's lives are often hell on earth, and they often seem doomed to become wards of the prison system. Consider this unedited excerpt from a letter to me about his horrific childhood from an inmate whom I met in TAX named Brian[5], and ask yourself what hope such a person has. The timid or sensitive reader is warned that Brian's description is explicit. You may want to skip the entire indented section that follows:

> I was born ... into a very dysfunctional household. I've basically been on my own since I was about 8 or 9 years old. Which is about the time I became involved with C.P.S. (Children's Protective Services). And from that point on my life has been nothing but turmoil. I've been bounced around from family member to family member, emergency shelters, group homes and foster homes until I went to T.Y.C.[6] at 14 yrs. old for U.U.M.V.[7] And once I was released from there, I was basically lived on and off the streets. I was around 17 yrs. old then. And it was during this time that I was introduced to drugs. Not so much as a way to hustle and stay alive but as a way to escape my past and present situations. So I became an addict. And after 4 ½ years of smoking crack, turning tricks and eating out dumpsters and any and everything else you can think of, I became a whole other person. All I wanted to do was die. You see Judge, when I first started getting high, it was supposed to had been a way to get away from my issues. But all that happened was my issues began to compound with my new issues (my addiction). Everything I was

17

trying to run away from only became harder for me to be bear. So I just quit running and just basically gave up. So I just started to live my life one day at a time. And each day as though it was my last. And Judge, since I've told you all of this, I just as well give it all to you so you'd know and understand how and when it all started... When I was a little boy I was about as happy as a little boy could be. I loved my mom. And at that point in time I felt loved by her. It was just me, her, and my little brother. Then she started seeing this guy who was a constibal. She married him just so me and my brother could have a daddy. And it was really good for a while. But then he started beating on my mom. So she left him. I guess he couldn't accept it because he sent one of his friends, whom he paid, over to where my mom had gotten an apartment, to beat her up and basically do whatever he wanted. Which is exactly what he did. I was six years old then. Me and my little brother ran in the room to my mom screaming. She told us to run and get help. But he caught us before we made it to the door. He locked my little brother in the closet and took me back in the room to my mom. He stuck the barrel of his gun in my mouth and made mom give him oral sex. She gagged and threw up on him. And that's when he snatched the gun from my mouth and hit me in the head with it. And right today I still have the scar. He then sodomized my mom. And when he was through he wiped the feces off of his penis on my face. And after he beat my mom unconscience he left. It was at this point that things between me and my mom changed. She started physically and emotionally abusing me. And I endured the beatings up until I was 8 yrs. old. Which is when I ran away. And that's when C.P.S. came into the picture.....

Brian's story is not unusual. I know for a fact that many inmates come from backgrounds like this or worse.

V. The Bankruptcy of a Nation

As a nation, we mourn and wail about the increase in crime and the decrease in public morality. Yet we refuse to open our eyes to see the cause of it. As a nation, we have become biblically illiterate and spiritually stupid. Our country has become morally and spiritually bankrupt. Ezekiel's rebuke to ancient Israel could be applied to our nation, today.

> Behold, this was the iniquity of thy sister Sodom, pride, fullness of bread, and abundance of idleness was in her and in her daughters, neither did she strengthen the hand of the poor and needy.
> Ezekiel 16:49 (KJV)

As a nation, we have an arrogant pride, fullness of bread, great idleness, and a great many of our churches do not strengthen the hand of the poor and needy. Oftentimes, we lament, "If only we had a different president. If only we had different congressmen. If only we had different judges. If only we had tougher laws." In our national self righteousness, we have forgotten an important, immutable, biblical truth: no man or woman can be trusted absolutely. Everyone can be tempted to sin in some way. The answer to our dilemma will not come from the government. The answer will certainly not come from one or a handful of better leaders. The people who make up this country have to change from within.

VI. The Old and Sure Foundation

The men and women who created our country wisely diffused power in a system predicated upon checks and balances. They collectively knew that we need to keep each other in check. Thus, the executive power, the lawmaking power, and the power to judge have been divided into three separate branches of government.

History has shown that whenever all or most of this power is reposed in one person or small group of people, the result is always tyranny because of the wickedness that dwells within the heart of every man and woman. There is only One in whom all three of these great powers can be reposed, and that is God. Indeed, in Isaiah 33:22, it is written:

> For the LORD is our judge,
>   the LORD is our lawgiver,
> the LORD is our king;
>   it is he who will save us.

Only God can handle all the power as lawgiver, all the power as supreme judge, and all the power as chief executive, and remain benevolent and loving. A discussion of the causes of the moral and spiritual bankruptcy of America could take an entire book, but its roots are invariably in our rebellion against God.

We live in a great country. Our Constitution and laws are great. Our Declaration of Independence is even greater still. It laid the foundation upon which our Constitution is based.

Consider what Edmund Burke had to say about the subject, "Among a people generally corrupt liberty cannot long exist." In the words of Benjamin Franklin, "Only a virtuous people are capable of freedom. As nations become more corrupt and vicious, they have more need of masters." Consider the words of James Madison, "To suppose that any form of government will secure liberty or happiness without any virtue in the people, is a chimerical idea."

Our second president, John Adams, said, "Our Constitution was made only for a moral and religious people.

It is wholly inadequate to the government of any other." The author of the Declaration of Independence and our third president, Thomas Jefferson, said, "Without virtue, happiness cannot be." Finally, that fiery patriot, Patrick Henry, said it well:

> Bad men cannot make good citizens. It is when a people forget God that tyrants forge their chains. A vitiated state of morals, a corrupted public conscience, is incompatible with freedom. No free government, or the blessings of liberty, can be preserved to any people but by a firm adherence to justice, moderation, temperance, frugality, and virtue; and by a frequent recurrence to fundamental principles.

Should we be surprised that what these great men said is proven repeatedly in each new generation? It is written in the Bible, "Righteousness exalts a nation, but sin is a disgrace to any people" (Prov. 14:34).

Gustave de Beaumont was a French magistrate and prison reformer. In 1831, he and Alexis de Tocqueville, who was himself a magistrate, were sent by the French government to study the American prison system.

When the two returned to France, Tocqueville reported on far more than America's prison system and wrote extensively on her system of government in *Democracy in America*. In volume I of his famous work published in 1835, Tocqueville observed, "There is no country in the world where the Christian religion retains a greater influence over the souls of men than in America."[8]

That is no longer true today. As a nation, we have become morally and spiritually bankrupt.

VII. Our Current Futile Efforts

I have seen come before me countless defendants who seem to have no moral anguish at the thought of stealing, falsifying a government record, or forging a signature. So what do we do? We pass more laws. Do we really think that harsher laws are going to promote future morality among the parentless children described above? Why are we so collectively daft as to think so?

We pass tougher laws as if that is going to promote public morality. Witness the Oxley-Sarbanes act requiring heightened scrutiny of corporate accounting after the debacles at Enron and a multitude of other companies. All of the honest men and women in corporate America are now saddled with heavier burdens. In this manner, we punish the innocent. Corrupt, greedy, self-serving people know how to evade the rules, and they will continue to do so. One of the principal results of criminalizing more conduct is the creation of more criminals. Yet nothing changes. "For it is: Do and do, do and do, rule on rule, rule on rule; a little here, a little there" (Isa. 28:10).

More liberal social programs will not make much of a difference, either. The problem lies within the heart of man, something that a program cannot clean.

There are liberal elitists in this nation who want to cram down our throats their belief that we are descended from apes, yet they refuse to allow us to learn the lessons that we might learn from the animal kingdom.

In 1999 (and again in 2005), *Washington Post* columnist William Raspberry wrote on a fascinating phenomenon that happened among elephants in the Pilanesberg game park in South Africa.[9] The elephant herd at Kruger National Park had become too large for the park to sustain. Park rangers took a two-pronged approach to the problem: they transported some of the herd to Pilanesberg, and they killed off other elephants at Kruger that were too large to transport.

What ensued as the young male elephants transported to Pilanesburg grew into adolescence is remarkable. They became like wild, mischievous gang members. They destroyed about a tenth of Pilanesberg's white rhinoceros herd. Using their trunks, they hit the rhinos with sticks. Other rhinos were chased and stomped to death. The young bulls were just plain mean. They also exhibited very aggressive sexual behavior.

The Pilanesberg park rangers had to kill some of the wilder juvenile bull elephants. Someone came up with the bright idea of bringing in larger mature bull elephants from Kruger. The technology to transport larger bulls advanced to make the move possible, as it had not been previously. The larger bulls quickly established a hierarchy in the Pilanesberg herd, and the mischievous violence among the young bulls decreased. The juvenile bulls' testosterone and sexual activity also decreased. The younger bulls also started following the older bulls around, as if they enjoyed their new mentors.

In the 1950's, a psychologist named Harlow conducted experiments with infant monkeys.[10] The infant monkeys were separated from their mothers within several hours of birth and put with two artificial surrogate mothers. One surrogate was made of cold, hard wire mesh. The other was made of wood and covered with terrycloth. In each cage, one of the two was equipped with a nipple from which the monkey could nurse. Even when the wire mesh surrogate was the one that provided nourishment, the monkeys spent more time with the terrycloth surrogate. Nurturing was apparently as important as or more important than food.

The isolated monkeys also exhibited bizarre conduct, sexual and otherwise, when they got older. The females that became mothers later (the motherless mothers) exhibited indifferent, abusive, and sometimes lethal behavior towards their own infants.

Why do we marvel that young mothers today who have had no upbringing at all are themselves neglectful or abusive to their children? Why do we marvel that young men today who have had no upbringing at all engage in senseless violence and irresponsible sexual hyperactivity? Yet the number of such people without any upbringing is vast. What is needed most for these people now is the love of God expressed through the human touch.

If we truly want things to change, change will only come about with the change of human hearts, one at a time. Jesus Christ can do for free what millions of dollars in social programs cannot do: He can change the human heart.

VIII. What the Word Says to Do

I am not advocating governmental sponsorship of religious organizations. That would only further corrupt the true church, and many parts of Christ's church in this country are pathetically anemic. Moreover, the government has no business in passing judgment on theological matters. I bristle at the thought of it doing so. Yet, the government should not be hostile to religion and faith-based programs.

If there be any barrier between church and state, it ought to be a picket fence, and the two should be good neighbors. In many places in this country, the true church has become anemic, self absorbed, and totally loveless. We coldly mouth God's word in our churches, but our hearts are often far from Him. We care nothing about being a "doer" of the Word as the apostle James exhorts us.

Do not merely listen to the word, and so deceive yourselves. Do what it says. Anyone who listens to the word but does not do what it says is like a man who looks at his face in a mirror and, after looking at himself, goes away and immediately forgets what he looks like. But the man who looks intently into the perfect law that gives freedom, and continues to do this, not forgetting what he has heard, but doing it—he will be blessed in what he does.

James 1:22-25

Indeed, the massive proliferation of largely ineffective social programs over the past forty years or so is an indictment of the true church. Were people in the church doing what they are supposed to be doing, the need for many of our government-sponsored social programs would diminish or even vanish.

It is for these reasons that I am deeply glad for the work that Pat Howard, Dub Pearson, and a host of others do to reach society's castaways with the love of God through Jesus Christ. I am also grateful to them for introducing me to prison ministry, and I am grateful to have had the small opportunities that I have been given.

I can do in prison what I cannot do in the courtroom. I can tell men the way of deliverance from themselves. I can tell them the Way to eternal life. It brings me true joy to bring the message of hope to inmates.

IX. The Sermons Presented

This book is a collection of sermons on needful topics that I presented to inmates over the course of about two and a half years. Chapters two and three are my journey to the faith, and in the faith, respectively. The sermons are set forth in chapters four through ten. Chapter eleven is the conclusion.

Many inmates have a deep hunger for the Word of God. Since my first meeting, men have asked me for my notes.

From that point forward, I made the sermon notes more detailed and brought many copies so that the men could study them later in their cells. Occasionally, I quote lengthy Bible passages in the notes because I know that many inmates do not have Bibles in their cells.

It is useful for them to have the relevant verses there with them when they study later. Although I stuck to the outline and format of the sermon notes, I did not read from them verbatim, and occasionally I would bring up other passages that came to mind and that fit the discussion. Thus, these sermon notes, when first written, were intended to serve as both an overview of the message preached and a tool for later study.

There is some overlap in the sermons. The nuts and bolts of the gospel are contained in each message. Each message is intended to stand alone. I never know who will be in attendance at the meetings. A man might show up for chapel who had never attended before, and it might be the only time I ever speak to him. The gospel is usually preceded by a discussion of the law of God. Many preachers and evangelists have abandoned this biblical method of evangelism: first the law, then the gospel. Many preach a "repentanceless" gospel which portrays Jesus as a cosmic teddy bear who just wants to give us a big hug. This makes for cheap grace and a happy-clappy, name-it-and-claim-it, prosperity gospel that may lead people into false conversions. Jesus Christ is God. He is holy, and we have to come to Him in humility.

The Scripture references in many of the sermons are detailed. I do not "dumb down" the message for the men because they are inmates. To be sure, some have a very limited education. Yet, some have very keen minds. I know one inmate who speaks five languages. Furthermore, all of the inmates have one thing in abundance that is conducive to good Bible study: time. God can open their minds and their hearts. "So neither he who plants nor he who waters is anything, but only God, who makes things grow" (1 Cor. 3:7). My duty is to plant the seed.

X. A Fervent Hope

It is my fervent hope that this little book will find its way into the hands of many inmates. I hope that they, by reading and believing, may know the truth and be truly set free, even if they are destined to spend the rest of their earthly lives in prison. I resolve to know nothing when among them "except Jesus Christ and him crucified" (1 Cor. 2:2), and I hope to help as many as I can to know the joy unspeakable.

CHAPTER 2

A Testimony, Plea and Conviction

—ɯ—

B efore the sermons, it seemed good to me to describe
my own journey to the faith and in the faith. Chapter
two is life up to the point of becoming a Christian ("B.C.").
Chapter three is life after conversion ("A.D.").

I. The Early Years

My father was a lieutenant in the Air Force stationed at
McGuire Air Force Base when I was born. At that time, my
mother and father lived in a trailer home in New Egypt, New
Jersey.

I can remember as early as age five or six having some
concept of God. When I was young, I was taken to church
(one that had uncomfortable pews) and, from time to time,
to Sunday school.

Of course, I knew the Christmas story: baby Jesus being
born to Mary and Joseph, wrapped in swaddling clothing, and
laid in a manger. What child didn't? After all, I felt Christmas
was the best time of year because it meant presents, a long
break from school, lots of sweets and other good food, and
playing in the snow (yes, I experienced snow in my younger
years). I had some vague and foggy notion that Jesus was the

Son of God, yet I did not understand this concept because I knew that He had Mary and Joseph as His parents.

I also knew something about the Easter story: that Jesus died on the cross for mankind. This was even harder to grasp, and I did not spend a lot of time wrestling with it. That is not too surprising when you consider that I was six years old. Although I liked Easter with all of the candy and the hunt for Easter eggs, I definitely liked Christmas better because of the presents. Besides that, it seemed like the Sunday clothes that I had to wear for Easter were more uncomfortable than those that I had to wear during regular church services during the year.

When I was about seven, my mother and father separated and were ultimately divorced. My sister, brother, and I lived with my mother and visited my father on weekends. I do not remember much about that period of time, other than to say I felt a deep sense of uneasiness. Perhaps it was the beginning of my insecurity. My mother tells me that after my father left, if ever she went to a neighbor's house for coffee, I followed her and waited outside by a window where I could see her, apparently because I was afraid she would leave, too.

Eventually, my mother moved my siblings and me to Houston, Texas to start a new life. Our first house was in Ponderosa Forest. I was in third grade.

After we moved to Texas, visitation with my father became limited to occasional holidays and long visits in the summer. In time, those too tapered off until we only spoke with my father every once in a while, usually around my siblings' and my birthdays.

During those early years after the divorce, I often dreamed of my parents getting back together. I suppose it is common for children of divorced parents to want their parents to get back together. I remember a family with a little boy who lived next to us in our first house in Houston. I have a memory of playing with him and telling him, "Your dad can be my dad."

II. Adolescence

Before my parents divorced, my father had become successful evaluating and recommending securities working on Wall Street. My father's financial success waned in the years following the divorce, and his support of my mother and us children likewise diminished. Over the next four years, our lifestyle decreased continually with my father's decreased ability to pay, and we moved from house to house, each one a little less comfortable than the previous one.

When I was in fourth and fifth grade, my family lived in a neighborhood called Walnut Bend. Divorce was less common then, and, to my memory, my mother was the only single parent on the street. My mother signed me up in Big Brothers of Houston. I enjoyed that a lot. My big brother, Steve, who was a volunteer about my mother's age, did a lot of fun stuff with me. He bought me my first rifle, a .22 caliber. Steve and the dads in Cub Scouts and Webelos were the only male influences in my life, yet they were not the same as having a dad around.

Prior to my sixth grade year, my mother, my siblings and I moved into the Georgetown townhouses near the current Beltway 8 at I-10. I missed my friends. My mother tells me that, at one point, she lost all contact with my father, and she eventually received no child support at all.

In the middle of my sixth grade year, we moved into an old rent house on Sheridan Street near a busy street called Greenbriar. It was close to the medical center in downtown Houston. This move would have been in January 1975.

The house seemed very old. It was cold in the winter. The garage was always damp and musty. Cockroaches were a problem, and I remember going to sleep on a warm night and feeling something climb on my leg. I brushed it off and realized it was a large cockroach. It gave me the creeps, and I could not go to sleep for hours.

Times were nearly desperate for my mother, my two siblings, and me. The oil embargo and energy crisis were in full bloom. My mother worked to provide for us. At the same time, she attended classes at the University of Houston to try to get ahead. She rode a bicycle to get to class, often through heavy traffic.

While I was still in the sixth grade, I remember being teased by other children at my school, Robert's Elementary School, about the secondhand clothes that my mother bought for me. They were all she could afford. Sometimes, the pants had holes in the knees. I became very reclusive. Oftentimes after school, I played with Legos for hours on end by myself and watched cartoons until my mother came home. I also liked to build and launch model rockets and play with model trains. I rarely played with other kids, and I was not involved in any extracurricular sports.

Sometimes, we had no meat with dinner. My brother, sister, and I hated the reconstituted powdered milk that we had to put on our cereal in the morning. I used to save what few nickels and dimes I could. Occasionally, I walked across Greenbriar to the grocery store and bought a large Hershey's chocolate bar. I came home and ate it on the porch. I broke off pieces of chocolate, dipped them into a jar of peanut butter, and hoped and dreamed that good fortune would come upon us. I thought of Charlie Bucket and his family in *Charlie and the Chocolate Factory*.

My grandparents on my mother's side drove down from Shreveport, Louisiana to visit us from time to time. When they did, they always brought a lot of groceries. I did not realize until much later that we needed those occasional bounties from Grandma Nell and Grandpa Jim just to have enough to eat.

The following school year was even more difficult. I was in seventh grade at Pershing Junior High. It was a tough school which had been desegregated only about five years previously. I had to take a Houston city bus to school.

I also recall having to walk a long way home from school on several occasions along Bellaire Boulevard in Houston, Texas. If memory serves correctly, it was a heavily trafficked six lane expressway. Later in life, my mother and my brother both told me that I frequently walked home because bullies at school often threatened me and took my bus money. It intrigues me that I have no memory of those confrontations.

Many of the students at Pershing used drugs. I remember a time when I cut myself sharpening my pocket knife one evening; the cut was so bad that it required stitches (you can still see the scar). I had to take my prescription painkiller with me to school. When one of my fellow students learned that it had codeine in it, he offered to buy it from me.

Perhaps the most disturbing thing that happened during my adolescence occurred one evening after my brother, sister, and I went to bed. One of my mother's female friends who had come by to visit stayed late after we went to bed. For some reason, I awoke and went into the living room to find them smoking marijuana. I was probably about twelve at the time. They made no effort to hide it.

I do not remember the conversation at all, but I was told to go back to bed. I do remember lying awake anguishing over what to do. We had seen vivid films in seventh grade about the dangers of drug abuse. I still remember a scene in a film that showed the face of a man who died overdosing on drugs. I was scared to death of drugs, and I believed that I should tell the police if ever I found someone using them.

I was torn. I reasoned that I could not call the police because if I did, they would take away my mother, and there would be no one left to take care of my brother and sister and me. By this time, we had not seen my father in a few years. I did nothing about the matter, but I was deeply unsettled and could not go back to sleep. I do not resent my mother for this incident – every parent makes mistakes – but this event affected me deeply. The primary authority in my life was doing something that all the other authorities over me said was wrong.

As things grew more and more difficult, the tension between my mother and me grew considerably. I was a very angry boy. The situation became more than she could bear.

In January 1976, the middle of my seventh grade year, my mother decided to send me to live with her parents, Grandma Nell and Grandpa Jim, in Shreveport, Louisiana. I resented my mother bitterly for it. At the time, I told her that I hated her.

I love my grandparents and have many fond memories of spending long summer visits with them even before I went to live with them. I remember lazy Saturdays fishing on Toledo Bend, and I remember warm times together at holidays. During an extended visit with them the summer preceding seventh grade, I got involved in the youth group at St. Luke's Methodist Church in Shreveport where my grandparents were members.

That summer and the next summer when I lived with them, I went with the youth group on an annual camping trip to Buffalo River National Park in northern Arkansas. Those were my favorite summers as a child, and I felt like a normal kid with regular friends.

I also have a distinct memory of my grandmother encouraging me to read *The Cross and the Switchblade* by David Wilkerson during one of my stays at my grandparents' house. Although I am an avid reader and was so even as a child, once I learned that the book had religious stuff in it, I was not interested. I can only imagine the number of self inflicted wounds and the grief I might have avoided had I yielded to God much earlier in life.

Moving in with my grandparents was a difficult adjustment at first, but I quickly came to love it. I respected my grandparents and loved them dearly. There was only one time that my grandfather ever spanked me, and I deserved it.

It was a joy living with them, and naturally, I became a regular churchgoer as they were. I also enjoyed the friends I made both at school and at church. Even in all this, I did not understand what it meant to receive Jesus Christ, what it meant to be born again. Yet, with the benefit of hindsight, I can see now that God was planting seeds that would take root much later in life.

While my mother and brother and sister still lived in Houston, my mother began dating the man who would become my stepfather. They married in December 1976, and all four of them began living in my stepfather's house in Stafford, Texas, near Sugarland. Stafford is in Fort Bend County, but it is essentially part of the Houston metroplex.

Naturally, my mother began planning for me to move back in with my primary family, and I moved back to Texas to live with my mother and stepfather in January 1977. I was in eighth grade at Sugarland Junior High School. I didn't know any of the kids, and I became reclusive again.

Getting used to living with my mother and having a male authority figure around was difficult. My stepfather was an ex-Marine, and I often thought that he acted like he still was in the Corps. I resented his authority because I had not had a father figure around for six years. I generated considerable friction with my mother and stepfather and between them during the next four years when I was in high school. I was very self absorbed, and I lied to my parents at times.

To his credit, my stepfather did everything he could for me, and he went to great lengths to help me. I know that he loved me, and he still does. My parents made me sign up for baseball over my objection the spring of 1977, that second half of my eighth grade year. My stepfather even coached my team, even though less than a year before that, I had never met him.

I had little skill at the sport, was embarrassed, and felt that my peers, who had been playing since they were in T-Ball, had a huge advantage over me. Up until this point, I had never participated in any kind of little league baseball, football, soccer, or basketball. I had average athletic ability and no opportunity to develop what I had. I played baseball again when I was in the ninth grade, but I did not enjoy it because I felt so inadequate.

III. High School

In 1977, I graduated from Sugarland Junior High School. I had a few friends, but none were very close at the time. I was somewhat of an outsider as most of my friends had known each other since early childhood. I was still interested in model rockets and oftentimes launched model rockets with other kids in the neighborhood several years younger than I. I was a chubby teenager who did not fit in very well among my peers at school. I was considered a geek. My few friends were a handful of guys from my neighborhood.

During my sophomore year, my parents had purchased a small ranch in Moulton, a town about two hours west of Stafford, Texas. That fact became significant later. Also, during my sophomore year, some of my friends and I went through a phase of shoplifting. My family was much better off than it had been two years previously before my mother remarried. My mother's earning ability had increased considerably, and my stepfather was established and respected in his job as a regional sales rep for a major lock company. Of course, by then I was also able to earn my own money, so we certainly did not need what we were stealing.

When my parents figured out that my friends and I were stealing, they made my friends tell their parents (or they would), and they made me bag up the stuff that I stole. They took me to the store that was my victim, and they made me turn the goods over to the manager and apologize (that was not all of the punishment that I received). I was ashamed. There was no good reason for doing what we did. We did it out of sheer mischievousness.

One form of discipline my parents imposed that has served me well was the development of a strong work ethic. I started working as a sacker in a local grocery store when I was thirteen and still a freshman in high school. I also mowed lawns to make money. Later, after my junior year in high school, my parents encouraged me to get a job on a Gunite crew doing swimming pool construction.[11]

The son of some good friends of theirs put himself through college and dental school doing Gunite work, and he was able to earn a lot of money doing it. When I started out working Gunite, I busted ninety-four pound sacks of Portland cement into a top hopper of the Gunite rig. Later, I worked as a rebounder shoveling the waste concrete out of the bottom of the swimming pool. It was hot work in Houston during the months of July and August. You might say I developed my work ethic in the bottom of a pit.

Eventually, I worked as the front end loader driver. In the summers while some of my friends were making four dollars an hour life guarding, I was making eighty to one hundred twenty dollars a day six days a week working Gunite. I had money and bought what I wanted. While a strong work ethic is good, excessive self-reliance can cause one to ignore God, and that was what I did.

The summer before my junior year, I became good friends with a guy named Jon. He lived in my neighborhood, and he was a year behind me in high school. He had played on the same baseball team with me with I was a freshman, and we sacked groceries together at the local supermarket.

He was a football player and much more athletically inclined than I was. He was dedicated to the sport.

That summer of 1979, he asked me to join him at the field house to lift weights. I was surprised at how much I enjoyed it. The field house was usually empty. Not many of the other players worked out over the summertime (at least not at school), so I became Jon's weightlifting partner. I began to lose my chubby appearance, and I enjoyed growing stronger. Jon introduced me to Coach Melton, the junior varsity football coach, and encouraged me to join the football team.

I signed up and began two-a-days that August. It was hard, but I enjoyed it. I was years behind my teammates in athletic skill; many had been playing since they were eight or nine. But I enjoyed being a part of the team.

During my junior year, I did not play often, certainly much less than I would have liked. Yet I was happy to be a part of the team, even if it meant being a blocking target for the first stringers at practice. Because I had started kindergarten when I was five years old, I was about a year younger than everyone else. Fortunately, in high school I was fairly big for my age and could hold my own.

Being part of the JV football team did much to push back my insecurities. I experienced a sense of camaraderie, friendship, and "belongingness" that I had not known before. I also found that I was more accepted by other kids at school, and I got involved in other student organizations.

During my junior year, my parents and friends surprised me on my sixteenth birthday and had a party for me. The girl I liked came. She was supposed to be my date. Instead of staying by me, she and another "friend" went off necking. My "friend" boasted about it. I was hurt and deeply humiliated. Later that year, I dated another girl a few times whom I was sad to see move out of state, but I did not date anyone steadily.

One of the student organizations that I joined was the Fellowship of Christian Athletes. There were many kids in the club who were truly committed to the Lord. However, there were many others like myself who treated it like a social club.

In the spring of my junior year, I came up with the idea to have a ranch retreat out at my parent's small ranch in Moulton for the FCA club. All of the kids had fun, and my popularity in the club increased significantly after hosting the ranch retreat. Ultimately, at the end of the school year, I was elected FCA president for the next year. Ironically, I was not even going to church at the time.

After I had moved back to live with my mother in the middle of eighth grade, she made a few attempts to get us all to go to church. That effort was met with considerable resistance and was soon abandoned. Yet, here I was the president elect of the FCA, and I did not even go to a church. I decided I had better join one, so I went to a local Methodist church that one of my neighborhood friends attended. I transferred my letter of membership from the church in Shreveport to the new one in Sugarland.

I remember the Sunday that I walked down the aisle alone when the pastor of my new church introduced me to the members. I was sweating profusely, perhaps because in the depths of my mind, I was aware that I really did not know what I was doing. Perhaps it was because I subconsciously knew I was a hypocrite.

As the soon-to-be FCA president, I was expected to go to the annual FCA summer conference. That summer of 1980, two or three fellow athletes went with me as I drove to the weeklong conference at Baylor University in Waco, Texas.

I was given a Bible at the conference. It was my first Bible, and I had absolutely no familiarity with it. I enjoyed the conference, especially the sporting activities and the food. I was exposed to my first concept of a quiet time because we all met early in the morning in groups (called "huddles"), then broke up for individual quiet time before breakfast. Much of what I heard at the conference fell on deaf ears. Often it seemed little more than lists of do's and don'ts. Yet I did hear some stirring messages and left the conference intrigued.

I have a vivid memory of my return from the conference that summer of 1980. I was visiting with some of my friends at the neighborhood pool about it. I have a distinct memory of contemplating, as I stood quietly at the pool, whether I could live life so totally committed to Christianity (not realizing that the commitment called for is to Jesus Christ Himself).

There were a few athletes in FCA that seemed exuberant about what they believed, and they seemed excited to do things that had a spiritual focus. Yet, I reasoned to myself that if I lived like them, I would not have any fun, and I wanted to have fun. I was chief among hypocrites.

So I entered my senior year college bound, enjoying being on the football team, participating in several other student organizations, and being FCA president. I proved to be quite a mediocre FCA president.

The conflicts I had with my mother and stepfather still waxed and waned dramatically. Who ever heard of a president of a Christian student organization who ran away from home? I did during my senior year while I was FCA president.

It was not uncommon for me to drink at parties as did many of my peers. I shudder to think of the poor example that I set and the people that I hurt by my self-centered and foolish conduct. Sometimes, I mourn that I was ever in that position because of my hypocrisy. Yet, in hindsight, I am now comforted knowing that God can restore "the years the locusts have eaten -" (Joel 2:25), even in other people's lives where I brought the locusts.

While a senior, I dated another girl for a few months, and I grew very fond of her. We were both inexperienced and stayed that way. I wanted to treat her right. She broke up with me and dated another athlete. I was hurt. I later heard that she became promiscuous. I grew cynical about girls.

That summer my parents let me stay behind while they and my siblings took a two week trip to Colorado. My excuse for staying was that I needed to stay in town, build swimming pools, and make money. They were furious when they came home and found out that I had had friends over for a party.

IV. College

The paths we take are often unplanned, and, looking back, it seems ironic that they led us to the place we presently are. I am grateful and happy to have graduated from Texas A&M University, but no one could have foreseen that end result at the end of my senior year in high school.

I had been awarded an appointment to the U.S. Naval Academy in Annapolis, Maryland. I had also been awarded a Navy ROTC scholarship which could have been taken at a multitude of universities. Having done reasonably well in math and science at high school, and given my fascination with building and creating things, I knew that I wanted to study to be an engineer.

That was 1981. I was seventeen years old, and I had just graduated from high school. Much to my parents' great disappointment, I turned down the appointment to the Naval Academy. They insisted that if I weren't going to accept the appointment, I at least had to accept the ROTC scholarship if they were going to pay for the rest of the bill. After I graduated from high school, my parents moved to their little ranch in Moulton.

One prominent reason that I declined the Academy appointment was that I wanted to be away from regimented authority. Some of this attitude can be attributed to the conflicts I had with my parents while in high school. Some of it can be attributed to rebellion against my father, who was an Air Force Academy graduate himself, and who had nearly ceased to be a part of my life.

Another reason that I declined the appointment is that I did not want to be so isolated from the opposite sex, either while at school or in the four year naval commitment that would ensue after attending the Naval Academy. By that time in my life, I had never had a serious, long term girlfriend, but I knew that I wanted one. Perhaps my desire can be traced to insecurities that I developed in my turbulent childhood, but as long as I can remember, I had a longing to be longed for. Thus, a major factor in my decision to attend a regular university instead of an Academy was that I wanted to be around lots of pretty girls.

If I accepted the Navy ROTC scholarship (which my parents required) and attended Texas A&M University, I would have to be in the Corps of Cadets and wear a uniform daily, unlike having to wear a midshipman's uniform one day a week if I had attended another university.

I almost attended the University of Texas instead because I did not want to be in the seven-day-a-week Corps at Texas A&M. I wanted freedom. Oddly enough, it was my avarice that outweighed my aversion to the structure and discipline of the Corps. I wanted to make it big later in life, and I wanted a high paying petroleum engineer's job upon graduation. Texas A&M is reputed to have the best petroleum engineering school in the world.

So in August 1981, I entered the Corps of Cadets reluctantly, and I managed to talk one of my high school classmates into joining me and being my roommate. The various outfits in the Corps had varied reputations about strictness (Texas Aggies call it "red ass"). I wanted one that was not so strict. As fate would have it, my roommate and I ended up in one of the strictest outfits. Not only that, my roommate let an upperclassman talk him into joining the Fish Drill Team[12], one of the most disciplined (i.e. "red ass") organizations within the Corps. He volunteered me also.

I hated the first eight or ten weeks in the Corps at A&M. In retrospect, if I had not been in the Corps, I likely would have applied no discipline to my studies. Had I been a seventeen year old non-reg (civilian) freshman, I quite likely would have partied all the time and flunked out. Surprisingly, after the passage of time, I began to like the Corps and especially the Fish Drill Team. They did much to build my self esteem.

Yet I was lonely and still had a feeling of emptiness. I did not date much, and weekends out with guys drinking beer got old.

I have a distinct memory from that first semester of my fish year when I sat at my desk one evening in my pale green, sparsely furnished Corps dorm room at Texas A&M. I looked up at my FCA Bible placed on the pale green shelf next to a bottle of one hundred ninety proof Bacardi rum. I had a sense that I would one day have a rendezvous with that Book. I knew that I would read it one day, yet I did not know why I felt that way. I wasn't attending church. I was not involved in any Christian student organizations, and, to look at me and my lifestyle, one would never have guessed that I had ever been involved in the Fellowship of Christian Athletes.

A significant event happened that semester also that resulted in my acquiring a new set of Corps buddies. Some sophomores in my outfit sought to haze me in a way that I refused to tolerate. One of them told me that I had to sleep under his bunk on a school night wearing nothing but a raincoat. I was not that easily bullied and reasoned that I was at Texas A&M to learn, not to put up with things such as that. Instead of reporting it to the chain of command, I just put in for a transfer to another outfit, and I was transferred into the outfit that I originally wanted to join anyway.

The tone of the new outfit was very different. At times, it seemed too relaxed militarily, but many of the cadets in it placed a great emphasis on study. Additionally, some freshmen in the new outfit were different, one in particular named Steve. He was like some of the committed Christians I knew in FCA in high school. He was not pushy, however, and we did not often talk about spiritual things. The subject came up once in a while, and Steve even invited me to join him at a *Campus Crusade for Christ*[13] meeting. I was not interested at the time.

I was still lonely in spite of being in the midst of an outfit of about fifty. Because my grades had been so good my first semester, I was not restricted to my room to study on week-nights as most freshman and sophomores are. That was a mistake, and I knew it. I even told the junior cadet scholastic sergeant that I thought that I still needed "call to quarters." He disagreed. Sure enough, without any requirement for accountability, I took advantage of the freedom, went out more, and drank a lot. Yet it was rarely fun, and my grades suffered that semester. In the spring of my college freshman year, I wrote the girl that I had dated a few times in high school before she moved out of state (she had since moved back to Houston, Texas). I never heard back.

I spent the first half of the summer after my fish year in the Houston/Stafford area with a good friend named Bill and his family[14], and I again got a job working on a Gunite crew. Bill was one of my best friends from high school, and he would later be the best man at my wedding as I was at his. Bill, Brian, Scott (my best friends in high school), and I went out a lot that summer, and I spent just about all that I earned.

Although I was terrified of drugs while in junior high, that summer I also tried marijuana. Perhaps it was providential that it and harder drugs were not more easily available to me. I dread to think what I would have done if I had traveled far down that road. The summer of 1982 was a worthless summer for me, and I was searching for a way out of my purposelessness.

When I returned to Texas A&M as a sophomore, I resolved to study hard, make good grades, and cultivate a new self discipline. Not long thereafter, I heard from the girl to whom I had written the previous spring semester. She lived in Houston, and was very interested in dating me again. She had been involved in another relationship at the time I had written her and had a child. Thus, her mother had not given her the letter that I sent in the spring of 1982.

A few casual dates led to a more serious relationship. I was soon spending an awful lot of time on the phone and commuting to Houston, sometimes on weeknights. So much for renewed self-discipline! I did worse academically that semester than the one previously. In fact, it was my worst semester at Texas A&M.

Yet, I felt that I was wanted and needed. My girlfriend's worries and problems became my worries and problems. I lost a considerable amount of weight because of the lack of sleep and the stress of the situation. By the end of the semester, I had brought my overall GPA down even further, but I looked forward to spending time with her in Houston over the Christmas break. But I was dumped and badly hurt. I felt betrayed, and I was very distrustful.

When the spring semester of my sophomore year arrived in January 1983, I returned a much more cynical young man. I started dating someone else, a girl whom I had dated once the previous summer when she was visiting a cousin in Sugarland. She lived in Dallas. I was more guarded this time, and I tried not to let the relationship interfere with my grades. But I still became deeply attached.

This time, I was burned worse than the last. My girlfriend was unfaithful to me (I learned this from one of her girlfriends who felt sorry for me). I was deeply wounded. I distrusted women completely. I had grown more and more self-centered, and I had determined that I was going to look out for number one. I was not going to let anyone ever hurt me again.

V. The Rusty, Dented, Steel Crucible

In the summer of 1983 after my sophomore year, my mother and stepfather required me to stay with them in Moulton and to work at a factory ten miles away instead of letting me stay in Houston to work, like I wanted. They had been quite disappointed in my nonproductive summer the year previously and my declining academic performance.

They also learned about the debt that I had incurred the previous school year accepting collect calls from girlfriends in my dorm room. Of course, this was before the proliferation of cell phones and dorm phones were not registered in any student's name. Students could not make or accept long distance calls. Another college student taught me a trick: I could accept collect phone calls, and there was no one that the phone company could bill. The phone company caught up with me, and I had to work out a payment plan to pay what I owed.

My parents were quite angry about what I had been doing, and about my declining grades. They took my car away and made me drive an old 1970 Chevy C-10 pickup. It had no air conditioning and only an AM radio. I hated that summer, but it finally came to an end. I prepared to return to Texas A&M for the fall semester. I was never at more bitter odds with my parents than I was that August of 1983.

I was scheduled to return about a week early to serve as part of the cadre to indoctrinate the new freshmen in our outfit. I had managed to pay the large long distance bill from the previous year, but I left Moulton with only about eight hundred dollars in my checking account to show for the summer's work. My mother and stepfather had paid for college costs that were not covered by the Navy ROTC scholarship the first two years I was at Texas A&M.

After the pitched conflicts between my parents and me, my mother told me that she and my stepfather would no longer pay for my college. She would, however, pay for one third of the upcoming fall semester in 1983, I was to pay a third, and my father was to pay a third.

I had no idea how I was going to stay in college in the spring of 1984. My mother told me that my father was supposed to pay for college for my siblings and me per the divorce decree anyway, but he had not paid anything towards it up to that point.

Because I had spent such a dreadful summer in Moulton, I intended to visit Bill and Brian in Stafford for a night or two before heading back to Texas A&M (Stafford was very much out of the way). As I headed east from the ranch, it started drizzling lightly. I was not surprised. We had heard that a hurricane was coming towards Houston. I did not pay much attention to it and figured I might get a little wet. That was all. I was driving into Hurricane Alicia.

When I was about ten miles to the west of Eagle Lake, Texas and the sun was setting behind me, I pulled up to a four way stop sign at the intersection of U.S. Highway 90-A and Highway 71 near a tiny town called Altair. In fact, I think that the intersection is the town.

I heard a strange sound from the engine, and then the truck died. I tried to crank the engine but to no avail. Even with the few cars that traveled that road, some were gathering behind me. Doubtlessly, the drivers behind me wondered about the delay.

I got out of my truck and pushed it with the driver's door open, left hand on the frame, right hand on the wheel. Another man got out of his car to help. I pushed the truck out of the intersection over to a nearby gas station that looked closed. It was fairly isolated, but it had a brick house next to it which looked like it had been constructed about twenty years previously. The date was August 17, 1983. It was starting to drizzle again.

Although the area seemed pretty desolate, the house was occupied by an elderly couple. I was irritated at the problem with the truck and had no idea what caused it, but I tried to be polite to the couple. They let me borrow their telephone, and I called my parents and asked them for help.

Moulton was about twenty miles away to the west. When my parents learned that I was on the way to Houston instead of on the way to College Station, Texas, they were furious. They told me that they had two children there that obeyed them, and they saw no need to leave a safe, dry home and come help me when Hurricane Alicia would soon make landfall near Houston. They said they also had to prepare the ranch for the coming storm. I thought that they were over-rating the coming storm, but, in any event, they refused to help and disconnected the call angrily.[15]

The gas station had closed. As it was now dusk, it was too late to get a mechanic to look at the truck, and too late, I thought, to get a tow. The elderly couple allowed me to keep the truck parked under the carport of their gas station. I slept in the back of the truck in the midst of luggage, an old trunk, and sacks of hanging clothes. I unrolled a dorm room size piece of carpet to make a crude bed.

The used carpet had been given to me by a neighbor in Stafford who had recarpeted his house. It was not much to look at, but for a modestly equipped college student, it was suitable to cover the cold, hard floor in a dorm room.

As I tried to sleep, I noticed that the carpet smelled like dog hair. It provided little cushioning between me and the dented steel of the pickup bed underneath. It was so uncomfortable that I could not fall completely asleep, but only dozed intermittently.

The wind blew erratically as the storm drew closer to Galveston where it ultimately made landfall shortly thereafter. The air was thick with moisture, and it drizzled on and off that evening. Because the gas station carport was so high, and because it did not extend very far out over the gas pumps, I was dampened with an uncomfortable mist all night. Occasionally, I awakened and went inside the cab. The bench seat in the truck was not much better, and it soon grew hot and muggy inside the cab as well. I was bitter.

When the next morning came, I called a tow truck. My truck was towed to a Chevy dealership in Eagle Lake. I wrote the man a check for the tow, resentfully spending some of the little money that I had. It took a few hours in the dealership waiting room before they could tear into the engine and even find what was wrong with it.

During that wait, I called, Dennis, one of my classmates from my Corps outfit who lived in Shiner, a town about ten miles south of Moulton. At the time I called, I was thinking about abandoning the truck, and I wanted to see if he could give me a ride to College Station.

He came by to meet me at Eagle Lake, but by the time he got there, I decided to stay and see if the mechanics could fix the truck. Dennis took several sacks of hanging clothes to College Station ahead of me. With the impending rains, I was afraid they would get soaked if I kept them in the bed of the truck when I drove back.

Finally, they told me what was wrong with the truck. The timing chain on the truck had broken. Because the crankshaft had turned out of proper timing, the camshaft had pushed on many of the push rods when it shouldn't. This action bent rods, lifters, and valves throughout the engine.

I still remember what the service manager told me, "Well, I am going to have to #%$@ you. You need a complete valve job." He seemed almost flippant about it. I asked him how much it would cost, and he quoted a figure greater than what I had left in my checking account.

I was downcast. I asked him if they could repair just enough to get me back to College Station. He said that some of the valves and rods were bent worse than the others, and they could try to repair just those, but he would not guarantee any of the work.

I waited patiently all day. I did not have a lot of cash with me, and I ate food out of vending machines. This was before credit cards were easily available to college students, and most people did not take out of town checks. I had a cheap dinner at a fast food restaurant across the street. It rained on and off all day.

Finally, just before closing the service manager told me that they got the truck in as good of shape as possible without doing a full valve job. I paid the bill – $243.43 – and I left. This time I headed west towards the sunset and back towards the intersection of Highways 90-A and 71 where I had broken down. I intended to turn right and head north to College Station and to skip the Houston/Stafford visit.

I drove about five miles. The engine sounded terrible. It clattered noisily, and I guessed that I was running on only three or four of the eight cylinders. Nightfall was upon me, the sunset hastened by patchy, thick thunderclouds.

I was pushing to make the truck do fifty miles per hour. I figured that there was no way that I was going to make it to College Station. I did not want to be stranded on the side of the road in a storm in the middle of the night, so I turned around and headed back towards the dealership.

By the time I got there, just about everyone had left. I parked the truck under a carport adjacent to and outside of the multi-bay garage where the mechanics did their work. I prepared for another fitful night of marginal sleep in the bed of my pickup truck on my bed of damp, old carpet that smelled of dog hair. I was miserable. The bright florescent lights that illuminated the dealer's carport all night made it worse. It was hot. Mosquitoes tormented me all night.

I hated the world, and I brooded over my bitterness. Having felt completely betrayed and deeply hurt by my last girlfriend, I did not believe that I would ever find a woman that I could trust. I was at odds with my parents and did not want to have anything to do with them. Although I had worked hard, it seemed like I could never get ahead, and I would always be without money. I was angry at God. I don't remember if it was the first night or the second — I think it was the second — when I shook my fist at God. I told Him that I did not want to have anything to do with Him if he could let these things happen to me. I was not going to become a Satanist. I figured that I would be my own man, my own entity, but I did not want to have anything to do with God. How foolish I was.

The next morning, I told the service manager that I did not think that the truck would make it to College Station, and had to turn back. I told him to do whatever was necessary to get the truck working so that I could get it back to College Station. By late that afternoon on the second day, they had finished the work on the truck.

I wrote a check for the second bill, a staggering sum of $556.20. This was more than I had left in my checking account. I realized I was penniless. Although my college fee bill was paid through the end of December, and I would have food and a place to stay until then, I had no idea what I was going to do during the spring semester of 1984.

I got in the truck and started heading west again. This time, it drove smoothly. I had a sense of relief, and although I cannot describe it, a strange abiding sense of thankfulness.

It quickly grew dark on the way home to Texas A&M. I don't remember if it rained much or not, but all the way back to College Station I contemplated what had happened, how life was going, and what I was going to do. The AM radio in the truck could not pick up any stations. There was not much else to do on that quiet trip but think. My hostility towards the world and my hostility towards God subsided.

My mind went back to that time between my junior and senior year in high school, when I had thought, after returning from the summer FCA camp, that if I were to become one of those committed Christian, Jesus lover types, I would never have any fun.

It occurred to me that I was angry with God for abandoning me, but I had never really given God a chance in the first place. And my life certainly was not fun. I put it out of my mind for a while, but figured I would think about it more later.

I arrived at Texas A&M in time for fish orientation week. My checking account was overdrawn and I had a negative balance of eighty-five cents on August 29, 1983. My hundred dollar monthly ROTC check for September was not in yet.

I called my stepfather and asked if he could lend me a little money to put in my checking account. He said no. They were still mad at me. I wondered how I would stay in school in the spring. I was embarrassed to do it, but I had to borrow one hundred dollars from my friend, Steve, another junior in my outfit, to cover the hot check and a few incidentals at the beginning of the semester.

Steve had always been a rock-solid type. He had fun with the rest of the guys, but there was something different about him. He was the one who had originally asked me to go with him to a Campus Crusade for Christ meeting with him, but I had turned him down.

Now, I asked if I could join him sometime. He said sure. I think it was providential that my dorm was about a hundred yards from the lecture hall where the Campus Crusade meetings were held once a week in the evenings. Had it not been so convenient, I might not have kept going.

VI. The Metamorphosis

So I went with Steve to my first Campus Crusade for Christ meeting a week or two later. At the meetings, we had a time of fellowship and singing, and then we broke into groups for Bible study.

I was in the first semester (new guy) group, which was taught by a graduate professor in mechanical engineering, Dr. Walter Bradley. That was providential, too, I am sure. I had switched majors to study mechanical engineering, and I looked up to this man. I had immense respect for him, and he had a lot of credibility with me.

I learned that salvation is a free gift from God, about our need for repentance, and about our need for a Savior. Like many Americans, up until then I figured I was a Christian because I had been told growing up that I was one and because I had gone to church a few times. I did not understand until then that it took a personal decision to believe that Jesus Christ was and is who He said He is, and that I need His sacrifice, His atonement, for me. Until then, I did not know that one must be born again.

Finally, I believed.

Like anyone who is honest with himself, I have done many things in my life that I regret and many things of which I am ashamed. I have set forth some of those things in this book. There are others that I omit to avoid hurting other people.

In chapter one, I set forth the terrible things I could have been. I thought about most, if not all, of those things. In God's sight, thinking about it is the same is doing it. As a man thinks in his heart, so is he (Prov. 23:7 and Matt. 5:21-28), so before I believed, I already was those other things.

Of all the things that I regret, the one thing that I truly regret most is resisting the Lord for so long, taking so long to surrender to His claim on me. Thank God for His patience.

One would be hard-pressed to imagine a feebler, more anemic prayer of acceptance than mine that fall of 1983: "Lord, if I haven't believed in You already, then I believe in You now." I prayed that prayer several times that semester, because it took me a while to realize that I had really believed.

My life has never been the same. That is not to say that I have been sinless. No Christian is; 1 John 1:8-9 speaks to that. But my identity is different. I know who I am and to whom I belong.

It used to trouble me that I could not pinpoint an exact date of my conversion like some people can. I can only narrow it down to a semester or perhaps to a few weeks. However, later in life, a fellow engineer and friend named Howard pointed out that "He chose us in him before the creation of the world to be holy and blameless in his sight. In love he predestined us to be adopted as his sons through Jesus Christ, in accordance with his pleasure and will— to the praise of his glorious grace, which he has freely given us in the One he loves" (Eph. 1:4-6). Thus, God knew all along.

It is written, "Woe to him who quarrels with his Maker" (Isa. 45:9), but my Maker was patient, kind, and merciful with me. Life is now a high adventure in which the work we do can have eternal significance. He has given me a wonderful wife, Carolyn. He has given me six wonderful children, but they are only the beginning. The blessings of God are too numerous to count, and he has truly given me an abundant life.

CHAPTER 3

Temptations, Trials and Tribulations

—✹—

J esus Christ came that we each might have an abundant
life. He never said that it would be easy. "We must go
through many hardships to enter the kingdom of God" (Acts
14:22). I would learn that truth over the next several years.
While it has not always been easy, and I have failed the Lord
in many ways, He has always been there.

I. The Honeymoon in the Faith

The first year after I became a believer was wonderful.
That fall semester of my junior year, 1983, I was changed.
Some changes happened immediately. Some happened more
gradually. For one thing, I had a peace and joy that I could
not explain. Life now had a purpose. There was far more to
it than the rat race I had been embarking upon.

One thing that my Corps buddies noticed immediately
was that I no longer cussed. I simply felt uncomfortable
doing it. I used to cuss like a sailor. Other changes took
longer. It took me several months to give up oral tobacco. I

knew that it was bad for me, and I now felt that I should take care of myself.[16]

I also had a contentment that I could not explain. I remember spending a Friday night that fall semester in my dorm room reading the book of Job, and it did not bother me that I did not have any plans. I made new friends that were very genuine, caring people.

Things were also difficult that semester because I needed to earn some money. I took a job delivering pizzas for Domino's. Working late nights while a cadet in the Corps at Texas A&M University and while taking a full load of engineering classes was hard. Yet, when I came home from work after midnight and put my tips and commissions on my desk – oftentimes nothing more than a large handful of change and a few wadded up dollars – I was filled with gratitude.

I went out on some casual dates with some of the girls I met in Crusade. I found that I no longer viewed them as objects. I wanted to treat them like ladies. Not that I am a great catch, but I also found myself not wanting to tempt them, either. In that first year I became a Christian, I remember times walking across the quad on a warm day when many college girls sunned themselves in their bikinis. I would avert my eyes because of devotion to God, and because I did not want to dishonor them in my mind.

Because I had become a true Christian, it seemed appropriate for me to learn as much as possible about the Bible. I signed up for a New Testament course offered by the Texas A&M humanities department in the fall of 1983. I took Old Testament the following spring.[17] I also became a lot more interested in people, generally. I found myself caring for people who did not have anything to offer me. I later took two additional humanities courses, "Near Eastern Religion" and "Indian and Oriental Religion," not because I doubted what I believed, but because I wanted to understand what other people thought.

Although I had never been more at odds with my parents than in August of 1983, our relationship over that fall semester changed remarkably. I remember my mother telling me during Christmas break of 1983 that the previous semester was the best one we had ever had as far as our relationship went.

That Christmas break in 1983-84, I also signed up for a Campus Crusade for Christ conference in Kansas City, Missouri called KC83. College students from several surrounding states attended, and we were treated with several great speakers.

One evening shortly after Christmas in 1983, I and many other college students boarded one of several chartered buses in Houston for the long drive up to Kansas City. On the trip up, I sat next to a wonderful gal who was a senior at Baylor. We talked until the early hours of the morning during that drive, sharing how we both became Christians. I enjoyed her conversation and the fellowship. There were several thousand students at the conference. I only saw her occasionally in passing during the conference, but we greeted each other warmly. I spent much of my spare time during the conference with new friends that I had met through Campus Crusade at Texas A&M.

There was a lot to do at KC83, and there was a lot of good teaching. Every morning a distinguished professor from Dallas Theological Seminary, Dr. Howard Hendricks, taught us in a large auditorium. Each morning he spoke on a different Bible character who was a revolutionary for God. One morning he spoke on Daniel. On another, he taught us about Shadrach, Meshach and Abednego.

The talks were very inspirational, and I found myself wanting to have that kind of devotion to God and wanting to make a difference in the world. It was about this time that I began to sense a calling for public service.

While my relationship with my mother and stepfather improved dramatically that fall semester in 1983, we did not discuss the matter of tuition and other college expenses that Christmas break. When at KC83, I did not have a lot of money with me, but it always seemed to be just enough. I was learning to trust God with my finances.

On the way back to Houston, I sat next to the Baylor gal that I met on the way up, and we talked again for hours. When we got back, we exchanged addresses and agreed to stay in touch.

Shortly before starting the spring semester of 1984, my father said that he would come through and help me with college expenses. I was greatly relieved, because I did not know how I could stay in college otherwise. This also proved to be a good thing because it necessitated that we talk more frequently and, over time, we reestablished a relationship.

That spring semester was even more wonderful than the last. It was my best semester at Texas A&M. I did very well, and I made distinguished student. My Baylor friend and I stayed in touch, and we saw each other a few times. She came to see me a couple of times, and I saw her up in Waco.

Because I was a new Christian, it was surprising to me that at times I was able to encourage her through some struggles, but I was glad to do so. We were very fond of each other, and our relationship was pure. I treated her as I would want my own sister to be treated. I was surprised and glad of the change in myself that I wanted to treat her that way, in a way that honored God.

I attended her graduation that May. After she graduated, she went on staff with Campus Crusade for Christ, and we lost touch. I mention this young lady in particular for a reason. Sometimes God brings people into our lives for a moment. Sometimes, He does so for a season. Sometimes, He does so for our lifetime. God used this young lady to enable me to trust women fully again.

That spring of 1984 also had a few disappointments. In January, I was made cadet sergeant major of my battalion. This meant that I would be the cadet commander for the battalion my senior year. I was very pleased.

Yet, after I returned from spring break, the cadet commander (a senior) told me that I had been replaced with a female cadet as sergeant major. No other explanation was given other than the Army military advisor for the battalion wanted a woman in the position. I guess you could say I was an early casualty of the political correctness movement.

II. A Spiritual Dry Season

In the summer of 1984 after my wonderful junior year of growth in the Lord, things got harder. It seemed like the honeymoon with God was over. That summer, I went to Ft. Riley, Kansas as an Army ROTC cadet, and I was far from my new friends. For me, it was a spiritually dry place. I got discouraged. I did not have the support structure that I had had to encourage me. I would learn later in life that this is a common experience for Christians. After the delight of their first love of the Lord, they get discouraged. They feel lonely. They get frustrated. They feel like failures.

I was losing my fervency. When one becomes a true believer, he always bears the fruit of repentance. One of the more prominent of mine was giving up swearing. There were other less prominent ones, but that was one that all who knew me well noticed most. I, like many Christians, was learning that there are some sins that we struggle with a long time. I struggled with my thoughts, especially about pretty women. I was still different from my former self, and the change was real, but now I often lived in defeat.

The following fall semester, my fervency continued to decrease. In the first few weeks of it, I started dating a young lady. She had become Christian years previously, but she had since become very worldly. I had her join me in church and Campus Crusade activities, but my self discipline waned. There were times when I went to church and wept during the service because of my lack of devotion to God. I would sin and repent only to fall back into the same sin again. I rode on a roller coaster of emotion. It is an anguishing place to be: to know the good that you should do, and to be unable to do it.

Because I had taken a lot of courses outside of my major, I had to take an extra year to graduate. The summer of 1985 (before my time as a fifth year senior), I took a job waiting tables at an Italian restaurant in College Station. Not long after I was hired, another pretty young lady, Carolyn, was hired on as a waitress at the restaurant. She became a prominent person in my life the following spring. Though we worked together, we were not friends at first. She paid little attention to me. I learned later that, at the time we met, she thought I was obnoxious (sometimes, I still am).

III. Crisis in the Family

That same summer of 1985, my uncle (my mother's brother), who was in his mid-thirties, was diagnosed with prostate cancer. My mother, my grandmother, and my grandfather were devastated. We all were. We hoped fervently that he would get well. I called him and encouraged him. I prayed for him and asked friends to pray for him.

My grandparents went up to Colorado and stayed in a hotel for several months just to be near him. But he did not get well. I was angry and anguished. I was frustrated. At times, I blamed myself. Perhaps my prayers went unanswered because I had so little faith. Perhaps they went unanswered because I was such a bad sinner. My uncle died in October 1985 on my stepfather's birthday.

I flew with my mother to the funeral in Colorado. It was heart wrenching. He left behind a widow and a cute little boy. After the funeral, we flew home with my grandparents, who had been by my uncle's side for the last several months before he died. I sat next to my grandmother on the flight home. Her son was very dear to her, and she wept much of the flight home. I did what I could to comfort her.

It was about that time that I broke up with the young lady I had been dating for a while. I mourned about that not because I thought it was a relationship that was meant to be. I mourned for the pain I caused. And I mourned for my lack of devotion to the Lord.

About three weeks after my uncle's funeral, we received news that pierced my heart like a knife. We found out that my grandmother had ovarian cancer. She had been feeling ill for some time while in Colorado, but we all thought it was due to grief and the stress of her son dying. I was devastated.

Once again, I prayed for her healing, and I asked my friends at church to do the same. She did not get well. Because she had seen what her son went through, she opted not to have chemotherapy.

We spent our last Christmas with her in 1985. We were glad to have her with us, but it was painful to think of what was coming. There were several nights early that spring semester in 1986 that I cried myself to sleep thinking about her. She died in February 1986. I was forlorn, and I felt like a rudderless ship.

IV. New Beginnings

A few months later, I asked Carolyn (the gal that I worked with at the Italian restaurant) to join me for breakfast after our shift was over (something we wait staff often did). I enjoyed the conversation, and I asked her out again to dinner.

She later told me that, at the time I asked her out to dinner, another waitress was interested in me. Carolyn's plan at the time was to go out with me, but talk up her friend, the other gal who was interested in me. Halfway into the date, however, Carolyn started rethinking her plan, and she decided that she liked my company and that the other gal was on her own.

That was her senior year, and my fifth year. We went to Ring Dance together that April. The brother of a husband of one of her childhood friends was a fellow A&M student. He was also a pilot who was trying to log hours. Carolyn arranged for him to fly us to Austin for dinner the night of Ring Dance.

When we left Easterwood airport to get into the private plane, I was wearing a tux and she an evening gown. A lady at the terminal asked us if we were newlyweds. We laughed. I remember flying back later that evening for the dance. As we circled over the Texas A&M campus, Rudder tower (which looked so tiny) and all of the lights down below on campus reminded me of the Peter Pan ride on the magic ship at Disney World. It seemed like a fairy tale. We continued to date, fell in love, and got married not long after we both graduated.

The Bible says that Isaac son of Abraham mourned his mother, Sarah's death. Yet, when he found his bride to be, it says he "took Rebekah, and she became his wife; and he loved her: and Isaac was comforted after his mother's death" (Gen. 24:67 KJV). To me, it seemed that God gave me Carolyn, and I was comforted after my grandmother's death.

Our lives have been a continuation of the high adventure. We both had our degrees from Texas A&M, and we faced the future with eagerness.

Right before my junior year in college, I switched from the Navy ROTC program to the Army ROTC program and took a Guaranteed Reserve Forces Duty contract. That meant that I would be trained like any other second lieutenant, but instead of going on active duty, I was committed to serve eight years in the Army Reserves or National Guard.

I had to wait several months to get orders for the Officer Basic Course (OBC) required for second lieutenants. Although I had a degree in engineering, I could not really look for a permanent job yet. My Army contract required me to serve about six months active duty for training at OBC, but I did not know when I would go or return. Few would be interested in hiring someone without knowing when he could start. In fact, the summer after I graduated, I framed houses on a framing crew for six dollars per hour even though I had a bachelor's degree in mechanical engineering. I took odd jobs, and I once cut grass at a cemetery.

Finally, I received orders to two different military posts at about the same time. The National Guard issued orders for me to go to Ft. Knox, Kentucky (the Armor school) as I was in the 49th Armored Division, Texas Army National Guard. The Army Reserves had issued orders for me to go to Ft. Benning, Georgia.

In middle of November 1986, we had all of our furniture loaded on a flatbed trailer that we were going to pull with my father-in-law's truck. I felt like Abraham packing up to leave Haran not knowing where he was going. Shortly before we had to leave, the Ft. Knox orders were canceled, and we made our way to Ft. Benning.

We did not know a soul there. I checked in at the orderly room at Ft. Benning the Friday before the Monday I was to report. We then drove around Columbus, Georgia, trailer in tow, looking for an apartment. Amazingly, we found a complex that had a vacancy that same day, and we did not have to check into a hotel first. The Lord had directed our steps.

At the time we moved to Georgia, my wife was pregnant. The delay in orders proved to be a blessing. Because she was pregnant and developed complications, I was permitted to bring her with me to Ft. Benning, and our first son was born at Martin Army Hospital (we would have had no insurance, otherwise). I undertook the training with eagerness.

In January 1987, I was urgently pulled off the M-60 machine gun range. I was very surprised because our baby was not due for several weeks. He was born prematurely after my wife started bleeding. Not only that, he had a knot in his cord. Yet the Lord blessed us with a healthy baby. Today, as I write this, he is a sophomore at Texas A&M and is a cadet in my old outfit.

After I completed IOBC in March 1987, we headed back to Texas, and I looked for a job in earnest. I went to the placement center at Texas A&M, hoping to contact some companies that were hiring recent engineering graduates. All of the recruiting for that year had already been completed by the time I got there in April 1987. I anguished over getting a job.

I made copies of business cards of the recruiters who had come in the previous six or seven months, and I started calling them at their employers' offices. I lobbied for interviews and went to where they were. The Lord handed me a dream job for a recent engineering graduate. I was hired by Rockwell Shuttle Operations Company at the NASA-Johnson Space Center, Houston, Texas.

My wife, infant child, and I started attending a Bible church in Clear Lake. Work was exciting and life was good. In November 1987, we learned early the anguish of seeing a child seriously ill. When he was only ten months old, our son contracted pneumonia. My wife and I took turns sleeping on the couch in the hospital room at Texas Children's Hospital. My wife's best friend, Lynette, brought us Thanksgiving dinner in the hospital. We had much for which to thank God.

V. The Long, Dreary Ordeal of Law School

Not long after starting my new job, I reconnected with my high school friend Bill. After graduating high school, he had commuted to the University of Houston (UH) and earned a degree in accounting.

That summer of 1987, he asked me if I wanted to take the law school entrance exam (LSAT) with him. He had wanted to go to law school since we were in junior high. I told him that I had a great job that I did not want to leave, and, besides, I could not afford to quit work for law school because I had a wife and kid to support.

He told me that UH and South Texas College of Law (also in downtown Houston) both offered night classes with the same professors. You could get the same law degree but keep your day job. Going part time takes four years instead of three, and you take classes in both summer sessions as well. He talked me into signing up for the LSAT, and I paid my fifty-five dollar filing fee. Our plan was to study for it together.

As it turned out, he had a schedule conflict and could not take the test when I was signed up to take it in October 1987. As I had already paid my filing fee, I decided to go ahead and take the test.

Without a study partner, I did not prepare much. I worked a practice exam the night before the test, then drove to downtown Houston the next morning. I remember praying in the parking lot before the exam, "Lord, if You want me to go to law school, You have to make it happen."

At the time, the television series *L.A. Law* was really popular, and law school applications were at an all time high. It was getting harder to get into law school. An applicant had to have either a really good undergraduate GPA and a pretty good LSAT score, or a pretty good GPA and a really high LSAT score. Although my grades at Texas A&M improved after I became a Christian (and I became more self disciplined), my earlier marginal semesters dragged my GPA down, giving me about a "B" average. Thus, my only shot was to get a really high LSAT score.

Well, that happened, and I figured the Lord was directing my steps. I prayed again "Lord, if You want me to go to law school, You have to make it happen." I applied to only one law school, the University of Houston Bates Law School. Although South Texas also has a really good law school, UH was state supported, and I could not afford the higher tuition at South Texas. I was accepted and started evening classes in the summer of 1988.

My wife and I found out that God blessed us with fertility, and we had our second son in April of 1989. He was born with two knots in his cord, but God again blessed us with a healthy baby.

We decided that my wife would stay home after our second son was born, which was about the same time we bought our first house. Going from two incomes with one kid to one income with two kids at the same time we were taking on a mortgage was really hard, but the Lord always provided.

Our third son was born in July 1990. He came early also, and I was called away from a drill weekend at my National Guard unit in El Campo when my wife went into labor. A month later, Saddam Hussein invaded Kuwait. The President authorized mobilization of reserve units that month. All of my fellow soldiers and I waited in anticipation and, as Operation Desert Shield wore on, we took steps to increase our preparedness.

Operation Desert Storm (the ground war) began on February 23, 1991. A cease fire was ordered four days later. I don't know if it is true or not, but I was told that our unit was only three days away from mobilization when the plan was canceled because the ground war ended so quickly.

Part of me wanted to be called up; I suppose most men wonder how they would fare under the ultimate test of a man's mettle: combat. My wife told me that if I volunteered to go before my unit was mobilized, the locks would be changed when I got back. I don't know if she was kidding or not, but I figured if it was in the Lord's plan for me to serve in armed conflict, He would make it happen. I know my wife would have supported me if I was mobilized. I admire the brave men and women who have volunteered to serve in harm's way then and in the present conflict.

Law school was a real grind. It was a test of endurance. All through law school, I worked full time, went to law school at night, and served in the National Guard one weekend a month and two weeks in the summer. Three or four nights a week, I got home from class between 8:30 p.m. and 10:00 p.m. I was tired almost all of the time.

By May of 1991 when I had a year left in law school and it looked like I would make it through, my wife and I discussed my potential legal career. We knew that a lot of the top firms in Houston (and elsewhere) work their new associates during grueling hours for the first several years. Given what I had been doing with work, the Guard, and law school, we did not want four or five more years of me getting home late several nights a week and having to work most weekends. We decided to try to move to a smaller community away from Houston.

Most law students graduate in May, sit for the bar exam in July, and are licensed a few months later in November, if they pass. Larger law firms often hire these recent grads in June with the expectation that they will pass the bar. In the meantime, these lawyers-to-be do not generate as much income for the firms because they are not licensed yet.

The bar exam is also administered in February. December grads usually take it then. There is a provision under State Bar rules that allows a student to take the bar exam before graduating if he is within four semester hours of graduation. Because I wanted to move to a smaller community (with correspondingly smaller firms), I figured I would be more marketable if I had my law license in hand when I graduated.

My wife and I decided that I should try to take the bar exam in February 1992 instead of waiting until July 1992 to take it with most of my peers after the May graduation. Sitting for the bar exam early meant that I had to take extra hours in the summer and fall of 1991. Shortly after making that decision, we found out my wife was pregnant with our fourth child.

The summer and fall semesters in 1991 were the hardest of all. Essentially, I was a full time student at the same time I was working full time as an engineer for McDonnell Douglas Space Systems Company (I had changed jobs in 1989, moving from the Space Shuttle program to the Space Station program). At the same time, my wife was pregnant.

During this time, we kept growing in the Lord. It was about this time that I finished reading the Bible cover to cover for the first time (it took me over two years). The Lord greatly blessed the effort. It was also about this time that I started listening to Dave Reagan on the "Christ in Prophecy" broadcast every morning on the radio. Through that program, I acquired a better understanding of the signs of the times.

VI. Stressed to the Uttermost

By December of 1991, I had only one four hour class left to take the following spring. I, like many other soon to be bar examinees, signed up to take a five week review course called "Barbri." There are other similar courses, but they all seem like you relearn in five weeks everything that you ever learned in law school.

At the end of that month, we received some hard news. My pregnant wife was having serious blood pressure problems, and was put on strict bed rest. The Barbri course was supposed to start two days later.

I had to drop out of the course so I could take care of our three toddlers every evening. Even though the fees are usually non-refundable, the folks at Barbri graciously refunded my money when I told them about my wife's condition. This refund was a huge blessing because we were living paycheck to paycheck. I was so grateful that I bought flowers for the ladies at the Barbri office.

A multitude of saints at our church came to our rescue. Several families volunteered to watch our three little ones. I dropped them off on my way to work, each day at a different house, and then picked them up in the evening. Different families brought us dinner every evening. It was like manna from heaven.

My lone remaining class met only two nights a week, but I still missed many nights. It was all I could do to play with, feed, and bathe the little ones. I was so weary. Add to those duties that my wife had to be hospitalized twice that January to prevent our fourth son from coming too early. She kept going into premature labor.

Finally, in early February 1992, our fourth son was born. We think we may have set a record because three of our children were born while I was in law school. My fourth son was born three weeks to the day before the bar exam. Even though by then some of my classmates had completed their bar review course and said that they felt ready for the bar exam, I had not started studying for it yet.

All during law school, we had used our formal dining room as my study as we did not have a dining room table. After our fourth son was born, I set up my Army cot in the study and practically walled myself off from the family to study for the bar exam.

Our new baby developed jaundice, which required that we have a bright florescent light over his crib in our bedroom. Because I had used most of my vacation time the previous December to study for finals, I could not take off time from work. I studied whenever I could grab a spare moment. I prayed fervently that God would help me remember what I needed.

The day before the bar exam, while I was stressed out to the max, I received devastating news: my membership in the Book-of-the-Month club was canceled because I had not ordered enough books (I think I still have the notice somewhere). I had to laugh at myself. God has a sense of humor.

After the bar exam, I felt pretty confident. The wait began. Meanwhile, I had to catch up in my one remaining class. I had tons of reading to do.

Finally, May 1992 arrived. The bar exam results were made available on a Friday afternoon during a National Guard weekend. This was before internet use was widespread, and you had to call a telephone number in Austin to find out the bar exam results. Cell phones were not common yet, and I stopped in every small town (it seemed) on the way up to Fort Hood to call the number from a pay phone. It was always busy.

I finally called my wife and asked her to try. She got through and learned before I did that I passed the bar exam. After she told me the good news, I had a solitary celebratory dinner of chicken fried steak that night at a Kettle restaurant in Killeen shortly before reporting to Ft. Hood. I was exceedingly grateful to God. He carried me through one of the greatest challenges I had ever faced, thus far.

VII. Another New Beginning

I made many trips from Houston to Fort Hood, Texas for National Guard training during those years. The drive took me through Brazos County, home of Texas A&M University.

Several times while driving through Brazos County, I prayed that the Lord would let us live there someday. In the same month that I passed the bar exam and graduated from law school, I received a job offer from a small but prominent law firm in Bryan, Texas named Davis & Davis (I am not related to the namesakes; people just thought they were talking to someone important when I answered the phone). My wife and I were delighted. We put our house on the market and had a contract ten days later.

We began searching for a house in the Bryan/College Station area. We found a small house that we intended to use as a starter. There are a lot of good churches in Brazos County. We found one, joined it, and quickly made friends with several great people. Our house quickly grew too small, and we built one out in the country about a year later.

Meanwhile, I was eager to get started at work. I think that the managing partner was surprised when he gave me a file on my first day, told me to draft an original petition, and I completed the task that same day. I was chomping at the bit.

A few weeks after I started, the managing partner, another associate, and I were having lunch at the Mi Cocina restaurant in Bryan when we happened upon a local judge and his bailiff. My coworkers introduced me to the judge as the new lawyer at the firm.

The judge suggested that they send me down to pick up some court appointments in some criminal cases so I could "cut my teeth" and get some familiarity with the courtroom. I earnestly wanted to do trial work – I knew I wanted to be in the court room – but I didn't really want to do criminal work. I came out of an engineering background, which is typically very conservative. I had a stereotypical view of criminal defendants. Like most people, I thought that they were part of society's problems.

I received some appointments, and although I did not initially want to do the work, I figured that it was not immoral and that duty required me to do my best. It was one of the best things that ever happened to me.

I quickly came to realize three important things. First, not everyone who is charged is guilty. Second, even if someone is guilty, he is entitled to a fair trial and a vigorous defense. And third, these people are sinners in need of a Savior just like me.

It really made me take a closer look at what the Lord did for me, especially given my turbulent youth. I realized that in God's sight, I was no better than any of these people I represented. Some may have done worse things than I did, but none have thought worse, and God sees the heart. I believed that the Lord was directing my steps in the work that I was doing.

Through no effort on my part, I was appointed to some high profile cases early on. In the spring of 1993, stalking was a hot topic for the Texas legislature. It enacted a stalking statute, and it was such a politically appealing issue, they made the statute effective April 1 that year instead of September 1, when most statutes take effect[18].

About a month after the statute took effect, I was appointed to represent a man named Robert who was accused of stalking. I was less than a year out of law school. Robert lived in a poor community, was married, and had two small children. He was a rarity in the apartment complex where he lived. Drug use and drug deals were common there. Women who lived there often had children by different men, and fathers were often absent or in prison. Yet this man really wanted to hold his family together, and he loved his kids.

A teenage girl, who I learned later was a gang member, flirted with him at his apartment complex and made advances towards him. He spurned her. Not long after that, she was caught taking a handgun to school. When confronted by the principal, she contrived a story that she brought the gun to school because she was afraid of Robert.

Perhaps some of the authorities were a little too eager to charge someone under the new stalking statute, because there were a lot of holes in her story. I truly believed in my client's innocence. Perhaps the authorities lost some objectivity because Robert was on parole. I had no choice but to try the case. I was really intimidated. This poor son-of-a-gun's liberty was in my hands! I prayed earnestly that I would do a good job for him.

The new statute appeared to have been hastily written. One of the elements of the crime required the victim to feel threatened (a subjective fact) instead of requiring that a reasonable person in the victim's situation would feel threatened (an objective fact). I consulted with my boss about it, and he suggested that I challenge the constitutionality of the statute, which I did.

Here I was, a nearly brand-new lawyer challenging the constitutionality of a statute in my first trial in a court of record. I felt way in over my head. That's not to mention that my wife and I were in the middle of building our new home in the country.

The trial judge denied the challenge to the statute. I felt a mild sense of vindication about three years later when the Texas Court of Criminal Appeals finally did declare the statute unconstitutional.[19]

I fought hard for the man, and the July 1992 trial ended in a mistrial with a hung jury. During the jury selection, I told the panel that this was my first jury trial in a court of record. I received a backhanded compliment from a juror after the trial when he said, "We thought you were lying about it being your first jury trial."

We retried the case the next month, and Robert was acquitted. It made the newspapers. Some prominent lawyers in the community sent me cards and congratulated me.

Robert still had problems, though. He had been to prison before, and he was on parole when accused of the crime. The parole board issued a blue warrant for him (that is what the parole board issues when a man is accused of violating his parole). He was accused of violating his parole by committing the same offense that we tried to a jury.

After the acquittal, I informed his parole officer of the acquittal, and I figured that Robert would be released. I also told his parole officer about all of the evidence that proved that the complainant was lying.

It seemed like the hearing officer already had her mind made up, and Robert's parole was revoked! I was amazed, and I learned early that parolees often get little or no due process. Robert's parole was revoked for committing a crime that a jury acquitted him of committing under a statute that would ultimately be held unconstitutional![20] I thought this was outrageous.

I still wanted to help the man. In order to challenge a parole revocation based on a violation of an unconstitutional statute, I had to file a post conviction application for writ of habeas corpus in the convicting court. I filed one pro bono.

Meanwhile, Robert's wife and two small children had to move in with an elderly relative in Navasota. Robert had been incarcerated continually since his arrest. Some folks in my wife's and my home church group wanted to help Robert's family, and we delivered some Christmas gifts for them late that year. Jeff, the friend who went with me to deliver the gifts, and I were utterly humbled. The elderly relative was on dialysis and was confined to a rickety old bed. The family's living conditions were nearly squalid. Their lives were so hard.

After a hearing on the application for writ, the trial court judge sent the case up to the Court of Criminal Appeals without a recommendation. The court denied relief. I was forlorn. The decision seemed so unfair.

By now, I was treading on the patience of my employer. I had already "cut my teeth" in court on several cases, and they wanted me to cut back on the criminal work to spend more time on civil cases, most of which settled. While my employer had always been very good to me, our interests were diverging. I had not expected to like doing criminal trial work. I could get passionate about it. I just could not get the same fire in the belly when settling a car crash case.

VIII. The New Law Practice

After much prayer, I started my own law practice in April 1995. Ironically, my wife urged me to start my own practice before I was ready because she recognized how unhappy I was. Oftentimes, the stay-at-home spouse would be fearful to lose the steady paycheck.

I struggled with feelings of guilt for wanting to leave. My attitude towards my employer was such that I wanted to be like Joseph in Potiphar's house, a trustworthy steward. Nevertheless, I finally resigned and departed on good terms, but I did not take much work with me. I did take a landlord-tenant dispute and a few other unusual cases, but that was about it.

My wife and I had four strapping little boys, and my wife was a stay at home mom. We did not have any savings, and we did not want to take out a loan to start the law practice.

I bought a walnut desk and credenza (which I still have) with a credit card. I bought a fifty megahertz 486 based computer and inkjet printer from McDuff Electronics on a ninety days same-as-cash plan. I bought a few office supplies with my personal checking account. A couple of lawyers who owned an office building in downtown Bryan had some space available for rent with a turnkey deal. They provided a receptionist (for several lawyers), office space, utilities, cleaning, maintenance, a coffee service, and a conference room.

That little landlord-tenant dispute case, which I had tried earnestly to settle for my client's benefit, went to jury trial in District Court five weeks after I started my practice. We won on several claims, and we were awarded my client's attorney's fees (most of which were still owed to me).

Within forty-five days of opening my law practice, all of the office debt was paid, and I never had any other debt on the law practice as long as I worked as a lawyer! Not only that, there were never any months (except the first one in practice) when I did not make at least as much as I did when an associate for the firm. The Lord sure answered our prayers in a big way!

I thoroughly enjoyed practicing on my own. I was a general practitioner, but more than half of the work was criminal defense. I never had a shortage of work.

In the fall of 1996, a lady came to see if I handled grand-parental visitation cases. I told her I had not yet, but would like to do so. She told me that she had interviewed several lawyers, and she had heard good reports about me from someone in Austin. I was clueless as to who knew me in Austin, but I was flattered. She and her husband hired me with the hope of being able occasionally to see their nine year old grandson, who was the child of their only son.

The boy's father lived in Canada. His ex-wife, the boy's mother, lived nearby in Brazos County, but she had become extremely hostile to her ex-husband and his parents, my clients. Once, these grandparents came to see their grandson play soccer (they learned about the game from another play-er's parents). The mother pulled her son out of the game as soon as she saw them and took the boy home out of spite.

The boy's father hired me a few weeks later to modify the visitation rights which were originally based on year round education, a program that had been discontinued in the boy's school.

All of my clients consented to my joint representation. In December 1996, when the father came down from Canada to stay with his parents and to exercise visitation with his son, the mother told the father the day before his visit that he could only see the boy in her house for four hours under her supervision.

The mother was clearly flouting court orders. We had her on tape, and the next day I filed the paperwork to ask the judge to prevent the mother from thwarting visitation.

I intended to file an application for mandatory injunction.[21] While I was talking to the court's coordinator to schedule some time, the judge got on the phone (much to my discomfort and awkwardness), asked me what I was seeking, and then said, "Oh, you need an application for writ of habeas corpus."

At a hearing that same Friday afternoon, the mother's lawyer argued that the application was premature because visitation had not yet been denied although it likely would be. Amazingly, the judge denied the application, agreeing that it was premature though she was the one who told me what I needed to file. I should have ignored her and filed what I thought I should, an application for mandatory injunction.

Sure enough, that Friday evening, the mother denied visitation, and we had to start all over again with a new application for writ on Monday. I also filed a motion to hold the mother in contempt. This time the judge granted the application for writ and ordered the boy to be turned over, but she carried the motion for contempt until final trial, a technique that weak kneed judges use to avoid making tough decisions to hold people accountable.

My client's Christmas visitation was cut from six days down to three because of this mother's contumaciousness. The judge gave my client no relief. He had to pay a big chunk of money just so he could get half of the visitation to which he was legally entitled.

This began a long series of delayed justice, denials of access to the courthouse, and a denial of my clients' rights. The judge had a reputation of being "pro-woman" (one of my female clients even told me so after the petition I filed for her landed in this judge's court). She never would enforce her orders against this mother.

My wife has told me that when people hire me, they get me body and soul; I sometimes dream about my cases. Well, I was passionate about this case. I anguished for my clients. I also prayed for them.

This particular judge had been rated unfavorably by two-thirds of the local bar association in a 1996 bar poll. She had a huge backlog, and to put it politely, was regarded as inefficient. She was reversed by the court of appeals frequently. Many lawyers wanted to see her replaced. I had represented a juvenile in her court two years previously, and I honestly think that her mishandling of the case set the child up for failure. He did not stand a chance.

After seeing her refuse to enforce court orders in this family law case against the mother for about eight months and deny my clients (especially the father) any semblance of justice, I started thinking about doing something about it. There are three district courts and two county courts at law in Brazos County. All five are courts of general jurisdiction. Hers was a county court at law. She was up for re-election in 1998, and the filing period was in December 1997.

In August of 1997, I called several prominent lawyers in the community whom I thought might be interested in running against her. I was still only five years out of law school, and I wanted more experience before running for judge. All of those that I called said that they were not interested. In September 1997, after my wife and I prayed about it, I made an early announcement of my candidacy to challenge this judge.

IX. The Hardest Storm to Date

In the meantime, in April of 1997, my wife and I had learned that we were pregnant again. Our youngest boy was now five. Carolyn had complications with this pregnancy also. Hardship struck in early November 1997 when she had a major placental abruption. I rushed her to the emergency room.

Her blood pressure shot up to around 200/180, if memory serves correctly. The doctor told me later that he was afraid she was going to stroke, but a drug called magnesium sulfate prevented it. The doctor performed an emergency C-section. Before and during the surgery, I was in anguish and prayed fervently.

Another lawyer and friend named Kyle rushed late that night to the house where I had left the four boys asleep. Many of our friends prayed for my wife, and I cried out to God to have mercy.

The surgery was successful. Our daughter was born nine weeks premature and was two pounds, fourteen ounces at birth. She had to be life-flighted to Houston. My wife, who was barely coming out of major surgery, only got to see our daughter's leg in the incubator before our baby was whisked off to the helicopter.

Our daughter stayed in Houston for several days, and then she was transported back to Bryan. Unfortunately, a doctor in Bryan feared she was developing necrotizing enterocolitis, a very serious condition, and she was transported by ambulance back to Houston. Finally, after several more days, she was transported back to Bryan. We finally took her home after five weeks in the hospital. She weighed less than four pounds when we took our baby girl home. We were exhausted. The Lord carried us through our hardest trial yet.

X. Into Public Service

It was December 1997. Although I had sent out several letters, I had not raised much in campaign funds (the part about campaigning that I dislike most is fund-raising). I had not even raised enough to cover the filing fee. I also picked up two primary opponents whom I was not expecting (the incumbent was in a different political party). I was ready to withdraw from the race before I even got started. I thought that I could do so with honor since two other good men had decided to run, and I had a premature infant at home. People would understand, I thought. I prayed about what to do.

Then, late in December, a doctor friend came up to me after church, gave me a check and told me that the Lord had laid it on his heart to give a campaign contribution to me. I thanked him heartily, but did not look at the donation until I got home. It was a sizable contribution which was just enough to cover what I needed for the filing fee. I saw the Lord directing my steps. I stayed in the race.

I campaigned hard. So many things fell into place just in time and in amazing ways. I and my two primary opponents were political newcomers. All three of us were fairly certain that there would be a run-off. I was absolutely amazed when I won the March 1998 primary without a run-off. God blessed me abundantly.

I had some time to gear up for the big fight in November against the incumbent. As things happened, the incumbent's husband took a job in California, and in August, she announced that she was pulling out of the race to move to California. I was unopposed in November 1998, was elected to a four year term, and began work as a county court at law judge on January 1, 1999.

I was awed by the responsibility. It is humbling. I often anguished over the decisions I made (I still do), especially in child custody matters. The staff, the lawyers and I also worked hard. We reduced the criminal docket by two-thirds in about eleven months. I received a lot of good feedback.

Our sixth child, a son, was born in June of 1999. We were very apprehensive that childbirth would take a heavy toll on my wife. The last turned out to be the most routine, uneventful pregnancy yet. God has truly blessed me with a quiver full of children.

Four of the five judicial posts in Brazos County are up for election in gubernatorial years (as 1998 was). The fifth is up for election in presidential years. Even as early as February 1999, a lawyer suggested that I consider running for the 272nd District Court bench that would be on the ballot in 2000.

The incumbent was considering a fifth term. He was considered by some to be liberal. Our county is very conservative. He had also made a lot of people mad at him for one reason or another. In following months, a few other lawyers also suggested that I consider running.

What they did not realize was that there was a huge risk were I to do so. I could not simply announce candidacy for the district court, keep working as a county court at law judge, and then keep my current post for two more years if I lost.

There is a "resign to run" provision in the Texas Constitution which meant that my announcement of candidacy for the other bench would constitute an automatic resignation of my current office. If I were to run and lose, I would be out of office altogether. I envisioned the ridicule that would follow if that happened (he should have stayed put, that whippersnapper!).

I was uncertain as to whether to run or not, as was my wife. I decided to pray earnestly about it. The first Friday in November 1999, I went to a friend's ranch nearby with a tent, a sleeping bag, a jug of water, a Bible, and a devotional, and I wrestled with the decision before God all night, dozing only occasionally. The next morning, my mind was clear. I knew what to do, and I believed God wanted me to do it. I would run for the district bench.

On November 30, 1999, I announced my candidacy for the 272nd District Court. Ten days later, the incumbent announced that he would retire. There is a holdover provision in the Texas Constitution which allowed me to stay in the county court at law for two more months until the Commissioner's Court appointed my replacement on January 30, 2000.

I picked up a primary opponent at the closing of the filing period, but I campaigned hard that season, harder than I did in 1998 (I personally knocked on over six thousand doors passing out flyers). I won the March 2000 primary, and I was unopposed in the general election. My first term as District Judge began on January 1, 2001.

I ran for a second term in 2004, which I won after a difficult re-election primary campaign. That story is so involved, it would be better told in another book. Indeed, time and space do not allow me to tell of all the kid illnesses and broken bones (some of which resulted in hospital stays), designing and building two houses, the hardships of raising teenagers, preparing for and running seventeen marathons (in one of which I had a severely ruptured disc without knowing it), two back surgeries, and many other challenges.

Yet the Lord carried us through every difficulty. The Lord is sufficient for our every need. He has fed me every bite of food that I have eaten every day of my life. The Lord is our provider. He is our banner.

XI. Hope for the Future

The abundant life is often not an easy life. I have had difficulties, hardships, and sufferings since I believed. Much of it was necessary for me to realize my own worthlessness apart from the Lord. Yet, I can attest that the Bible is truthful where it says, "If we are faithless, he will remain faithful, for he cannot disown himself" (2 Tim. 2:13). We can also attest that He is truthful when He says, "Never will I leave you; never will I forsake you" (Heb. 13:5). The abundant life is a high adventure, and added to all that, we get heaven in the presence of God at the end. The blessings of God are too numerous to count.

In these latter years of my pilgrimage in the Lord, I have discovered many overlooked treasures in the writings of godly men and women who lived and died long ago, people like John Bunyan, F.B. Meyer, Watchman Nee, St. Augustine, Jessie Penn-Lewis, Andrew Murray, Jonathan Edwards, and others. One of my favorites is Oswald Chambers, a Scottish pastor and Bible teacher who died during World War I in Zeitoun, Egypt where he ministered to the English, Australian, and New Zealand troops. He is best known for the popular devotional *My Utmost for His Highest*. The devotional for February 15th reads:

> How many of us are willing to spend every ounce of nervous energy, of mental, moral and spiritual energy we have for Jesus Christ? That is the meaning of a witness in God's sense of the word. It takes time, be patient with yourself. God has left us on the earth—what for? To be saved and sanctified? No, to be at it for Him. Am I willing to be broken bread and poured-out wine for Him? To be spoilt for this age, for this life, to be spoilt from every standpoint but one—saving as I can disciple men and women to the Lord Jesus Christ. My life as a worker is the way I say "thank you" to God for His unspeakable salvation.[22]

While I mourn over my many shortcomings and failures in service for the Lord, I hope that He accepts my humble book as an effort "to be at it for Him." I offer it in faith as an expression of sheer gratitude for what He has done for me.

Most people have personal problems. Most of those problems are because people think too much of themselves, or they think too little of themselves, that God could not possibly love them. In the first instance, a person exhibits the greatest of sins, the sin of Satan himself, pride. In the second instance, when a person thinks too little of himself, he is also exhibiting the greatest of sins, pride. That person sits in judgment of the grace of God and the love of God, and he thinks that neither are great enough to overcome the greatness of his sin.

Jesus wept over Jerusalem. He also said of it, "How often I have longed to gather your children together, as a hen gathers her chicks under her wings, but you were not willing" (Matt. 23:37). Those who choose hell for themselves do so not withstanding the fact that God longs for them to accept His salvation.

As for myself, I know that I am worthless apart from the grace of God and the love of Jesus Christ. Yet, that does not mean that I have no worth, for it is written, "How great is the love the Father has lavished on us, that we should be called children of God! And that is what we are!" (1 John 3:1). Thus, I also know that I have great worth because I am a child of God. To the average person, that sounds arrogant, but there is no arrogance in it. It was not my doing. I did nothing to earn it. It was a work of the sovereign King of the Universe. I simply believed with the faith by which He enabled me to believe. I take credit for nothing, and God owed me nothing when He saved me.

True conversion brings forth fruit in keeping with repentance, which often includes the forsaking of obvious sins. Yet, Christians also often have other sins with which they struggle for a long time. I can attest to that.

There have been many times in my life after conversion when I have anguished before God about my thoughts. There have been times when I have wrestled through "the dark night of soul." At times, I have wondered "Am I really a Christian? How could I do such things!? How could I think such thoughts!?" I worked myself up into a mental pretzel where I thought about the hereafter and wondered "Do I really believe? What if I deceive myself, and only believe that I believe though I am not a true believer?" I finally got to the point where I cried out, "Lord, I give up! Save me!" which is where I should have been all along.

After many years, I realize now that God sometimes allows these struggles to bring us to the point of complete surrender. God brings us to the point where we must agree with Paul that "I know that in me (that is, in my flesh,) dwelleth no good thing: for to will is present with me; but how to perform that which is good I find not" (Rom. 7:18 KJV).

Although I am born again, I still long to get to the point in my walk with the Lord where I have what Hudson Taylor called the "exchanged life."[23] While I know that I am not there yet, I also know that the best is yet to come!

CHAPTER 4

The Unclaimed Pardon Free for the Taking

Presented by Rick Davis August 8, 2006
during Chapel service at the Hamilton Unit, Bryan, Texas.[24]

———ɯɯ———

I. Introductions

Friends, before we begin the primary message, I want to introduce myself. You know that I am a district judge. Before that, I practiced law with an emphasis on criminal defense work. Before I practiced law, I was like most people in society in that I did not think a whole lot about the criminal justice system or those who were behind bars. I favored tough prosecution of violations of the law, and I didn't really care about what happened to the convicts. Yet long before I went to law school, when I was nineteen years old, I became a Christian. I tell you this so that you will know that even though I did not care, I should have. In Isaiah 42:6-7, when God was speaking of the coming Messiah, Jesus, he said:

I, the LORD, have called you in righteousness; I will take hold of your hand. I will keep you and will make you to be a covenant for the people and a light for the Gentiles, to open eyes that are blind, to free captives from prison and to release from the dungeon those who sit in darkness.

Clearly, God cares about those held in prison. One of the best things that ever happened to me in my professional life was practicing criminal defense law. I came to appreciate deeply three important truths. First, not everyone who is charged is guilty. Second, even the guilty are entitled to fair representation, a fair trial, and a vigorous defense. Third, and most importantly, these men and women are sinners in need of a Savior, just like me.

Thus, at the outset, I want to say that I was a sinner in need of a Savior just like some of you still are. I am no better than any of you. One of my favorite authors is Oswald Chambers, a great missionary to the English and Australian troops during World War I. He was a committed servant of the Lord who is best known for his work *My Utmost for His Highest*, the world's most popular devotional. In the devotional for June 1st, Chambers wrote:

When God wants to show you what human nature is like apart from Himself, He has to show it [to] you in yourself. If the Spirit of God has given you a vision of what you are apart from the grace of God (and He only does it when His Spirit is at work), you know there is no criminal who is half so bad in actuality as you know yourself to be in possibility. My "grave" has been opened by God and "I know that in me (that is, in my flesh) dwelleth no good thing." God's Spirit continually reveals what human nature is like apart from His grace.[25]

Chambers was exactly right. Do you see what this means, men? God sees my thought life. No matter what any of you have done to get yourselves here, no matter how bad the crime, I know in my heart of hearts that I am no better than any of you. I was a vile sinner in desperate need of a Savior. Thus, when you hear this message, don't think of me as a district judge. I am one spiritual beggar telling another where to find bread. My fervent hope and prayer is that this message blesses you, and that you receive it in the spirit in which it is given. That is, receive it from one who has been humbled by God, broken by His law, and saved by His grace.

II. The Purpose of the Law

Now I come to the main message. First, let's examine the Word of God to see the purpose of God's law. God's law was not written to provide us with a checklist of things to do. As it is written, "We know that the law is good if one uses it properly" (1 Tim. 1:8). So what is the proper use of the law? Let's take a look at chapter three of the apostle Paul's letter to the Galatians:

Brothers, let me take an example from everyday life. Just as no one can set aside or add to a human cove-nant that has been duly established, so it is in this case. The promises were spoken to Abraham and to his seed. The Scripture does not say "and to seeds," meaning many people, but "and to your seed," meaning one person, who is Christ. What I mean is this: The law, introduced 430 years later, does not set aside the covenant previously established by God and thus do away with the promise. For if the inheritance depends on the law, then it no longer depends on a promise; but God in his grace gave it to Abraham through a promise.

What, then, was the purpose of the law? It was added because of transgressions until the Seed to whom the promise referred had come. The law was put into effect through angels by a mediator. A mediator, however, does not represent just one party; but God is one.

Is the law, therefore, opposed to the promises of God? Absolutely not! For if a law had been given that could impart life, then righteousness would certainly have come by the law. But the Scripture declares that the whole world is a prisoner of sin, so that what was promised, being given through faith in Jesus Christ, might be given to those who believe.

Before this faith came, we were held prisoners by the law, locked up until faith should be revealed. So the law was put in charge to lead us to Christ that we might be justified by faith. Now that faith has come, we are no longer under the supervision of the law.

Galatians 3:15-25

Paul also tells us in Romans 7:13, "The law is holy, and the commandment is holy, righteous and good." And we also see in Psalm 19:7, "The law of the LORD is perfect, reviving the soul."

That's from the NIV. The NKJV translates this same verse: "The law of the LORD is perfect, converting the soul." What is it that revives or converts the soul? Why, Scripture is very clear: it is the law of the Lord. Yet, we saw in Galatians that the law holds us as prisoner. Also, the apostle Paul, when writing to the Corinthians, said that the law (or letter) kills. In 2 Corinthians 3:6-7, Paul wrote:

He has made us competent as ministers of a new covenant—not of the letter but of the Spirit; for the letter
kills, but the Spirit gives life. Now if the ministry
that brought death, which was engraved in letters on
stone, came with glory, so that the Israelites could
not look steadily at the face of Moses because of its
glory, fading though it was, will not the ministry of
the Spirit be even more glorious?

So, how is it that the law of God can revive or convert
the soul, yet at the same time, as Paul says, it holds us prisoner, it kills, and it is a ministry of death?

God's law awakens our conscience on the one hand, yet
makes us painfully and dreadfully aware of the holiness of
God and his righteous requirements on the other hand.

It makes us aware of our inability to live up to God's
holiness. The law of God also makes us aware of our crying
need for a Savior. When the law does its intended purpose in
our hearts, in our minds, and in our lives, it drives us to our
knees so that we cry out, "Lord save me! I give up. Please
have mercy on me!" And it is at that point, when we come
to the Lord in humility, that He gives us the gift of faith in
the Lord Jesus. It pleases God to bring glory to Himself by
saving us through faith in Jesus Christ. That is when we are
truly born again.

Much of modern Christianity and many churches have
forgotten this powerful and necessary truth about the important function of God's law. Jesus is often preached as the
great life enhancer. "Give your heart to Jesus and He will
give you love, joy, peace, and happiness. He will heal your
drinking problem, your drug problem, your marital problem,
your problem with anger," and so forth.

To be sure, faith in Jesus Christ changes us from the
inside out, but we have to come to Jesus in humility with
a humble heart. Many people preach "cheap grace," grace

with no cost, grace without commitment, because they don't allow the law of God to do its work in breaking us and driving us to our knees.

With the law of God, God breaks the hard heart. With the gospel, God heals the broken heart. After David sinned against God and man, committed adultery, and then tried to cover it up by committing murder, he was crushed to the very core by the rebuke of the prophet Nathan. When David realized what he had done, he cried out to God for mercy. He wrote in Psalm 51:10-17 (NKJV):

> Create in me a clean heart, O God, and renew a stead-fast spirit within me. Do not cast me away from your presence, and do not take Your Holy Spirit from me. Restore to me the joy of your salvation, and uphold me by your generous Spirit. Then I will teach transgressors your ways, and sinners shall be converted to you. Deliver me from the guilt of bloodshed, O God, the God of my salvation, and my tongue shall sing aloud of your righteousness. O Lord, open my lips, and my mouth shall show forth Your praise. For you do not desire sacrifice, or else I would give it; You do not delight in burnt offering. The sacrifices of God are a broken spirit, a broken and a contrite heart– these, O God, You will not despise.

You see, the whole world is caught under a spell, a lie of Satan: that we must do good. That is the fundamental meaning of what happened when Adam ate of the tree of knowledge of good and evil. We know that we should do good. The problem is that we cannot do good. We can never act with perfect holiness and without sin, which is what the holiness of God requires.

Ask most people, at least in this country, if they think they will go to heaven, and they will say, "Sure, I've lived a pretty good life." And they will tell you about the good things that they have done and the bad things that they have not done.

But three of the most prominent godly men in the Bible were murderers. Moses murdered an Egyptian. King David committed adultery with a loyal friend's wife, and when she became pregnant, David arranged to have the man killed so he could marry the widow without anyone knowing about the adultery. Finally, the apostle Paul twice admitted that he was a persecutor of the church, and he stood by giving his approval when the Jews killed Stephen the disciple.

How great is the love of our Lord Jesus Christ! His grace and glory are magnified by how wretched a man He can save and redeem! In Paul's case, the Lord turned the greatest enemy of the church into one of the greatest and most devoted apostles. And all the evil things that these men did were washed away by the blood of Jesus Christ.

To see the mindset of the world, let us consider the man in Matthew 19:16-22.

> Now a man came up to Jesus and asked, "Teacher, what good thing must I do to get eternal life?" "Why do you ask me about what is good?" Jesus replied. "There is only One who is good. If you want to enter life, obey the commandments." "Which ones?" the man inquired. Jesus replied, "'Do not murder, do not commit adultery, do not steal, do not give false testimony, honor your father and mother, and love your neighbor as yourself.'" "All these I have kept," the young man said. "What do I still lack?" Jesus answered, "If you want to be perfect, go, sell your possessions and give to the poor, and you will have treasure in heaven. Then come, follow me." When the young man heard this, he went away sad, because he had great wealth.

Men, this passage speaks volumes. The man asked, "What good things must I do?" This is the way the world thinks. The whole world thinks that if we do good, we will go to heaven.

The truth is, we know the difference between good and evil. We know what we should do, but we cannot do it. Jesus challenged the man with the law, that is, the Ten Commandments.

The man was quite content with himself that he had obeyed all of the commandments. What did Jesus start with? The Lord started with those commandments to which obedience is obvious for all to see.

All of the man's friends could attest that he had honored his father and mother. But Jesus went further, because He sees the heart. When Jesus told the man what he still had to do, Jesus did not give the man a checklist of deeds (remember that we cannot do good). He told him to give up his idol, which was his wealth. The man could perhaps truthfully say that he had obeyed the commandments that govern how man deals with man, but his god was his money. He constantly violated the first and second commandments.

Friends, if I examine myself and you examine yourself in the light of the Ten Commandments, you and I can see that we deserve hell. We deserve God's eternal punishment.

Do you see that with the law of God, God shows us our true selves, that we are wretched, sinful, and evil? We fall far short of God's glory and holiness.

While the Lord is and was the perfect picture of God's love, mercy, and tenderness, we are sorely mistaken if we ignore that he also showed His righteous indignation with the proud of heart. In James 4:6, it is written, "God opposes the proud but gives grace to the humble." In Matthew 23, Jesus rebuked the Pharisees: the legalistic, religious hypocrites of his day. That chapter contains one woe after another. In Matthew 23:23 (NKJV), the Lord said:

Woe to you, scribes and Pharisees, hypocrites! For you pay tithe of mint and anise and cummin, and have neglected the weightier matters of the law: justice and mercy and faith.[26] These you ought to have done, without leaving the others undone.

Think about what the Lord meant here. What are the weightier matters of the law? Justice, mercy, and faith are. The holiness of God is so great that His justice requires sin to be punished wherever it is found. And because the justice of God is so thorough, so complete, so overwhelming, and so dreadful, we see that we are in desperate need of the mercy of God. And how is it that we obtain the mercy of God? We obtain it by faith in Jesus Christ. Thus, we have the weightier matters of the law: justice, mercy, and faith. As Paul said in Romans 3:21-28:

But now a righteousness from God, apart from law, has been made known, to which the Law and the Prophets testify. This righteousness from God comes through faith in Jesus Christ to all who believe. There is no difference, for all have sinned and fall short of the glory of God, and are justified freely by his grace through the redemption that came by Christ Jesus. God presented him as a sacrifice of atonement, through faith in his blood. He did this to demonstrate his justice, because in his forbearance he had left the sins committed beforehand unpunished— he did it to demonstrate his justice at the present time, so as to be just and the one who justifies those who have faith in Jesus.

Where, then, is boasting? It is excluded. On what principle? On that of observing the law? No, but on that of faith. For we maintain that a man is justified by faith apart from observing the law.

In Romans 3:19-20, it is written: "Now we know that whatever the law says, it says to those who are under the law, so that every mouth may be silenced and the whole world held accountable to God. Therefore no one will be declared righteous in his sight by observing the law; rather, through the law we become *conscious of sin*" (emphasis added).

Consider also how Jesus spoke to people. To the proud, he gave the law so that they could see their helplessness and neediness. To the humble, he gave the gospel, the good news. The humble he received by their faith in Him. Look at John 4 and the woman at the well who had had five husbands and was living with a sixth man not her husband. She was not proud. When He confronted her with the truth about her immoral lifestyle, she acknowledged Him to be from God, and she and many in her village were saved. The same was true of the woman caught in adultery in John 8. "He straightened up and asked her 'Woman, where are they? Has no one condemned you?' 'No one, sir,' she said. 'Then neither do I condemn you,' Jesus declared. 'Go now and leave your life of sin'" (John 8:10-11).

Do you see what this means, men? Because I have seen myself in the light of God's law, I can truthfully say that I am no better than any one of you. This is not false humility, for I know that no matter what you have done, no matter how horrible the crime was that got you here, none of you have done anything worse than I am capable of thinking. Thus, you and I, without the salvation of Jesus Christ, are identically the same: sinners condemned and worthy of hell. Without Jesus, we are damned.

Here is the good news: "Whoever believes in him is not condemned, but whoever does not believe stands condemned already because he has not believed in the name of God's one and only Son" (John 3:18). Do you see, men, that no one goes to hell for some major sin that he has committed? We were all condemned already because of our sinful nature. The holiness of God is so great that one single sin is enough to make us deserving of hell. Praise God for His salvation through faith in Jesus Christ!

III. Our Crying Need for a Pardon

Before we believe in Jesus Christ, we are in desperate need of a pardon. Now you all probably did not expect to hear a sermon that included a court case in it, but I am going to tell you about a court case that illustrates a very, very important truth.

Back in the early 1830s, a mail clerk named George Wilson killed his co-worker and tied himself up to make it appear that a robbery had occurred. However, during routine questioning, a few flaws were found in his statements, and he ultimately broke down and confessed to the murder. He was tried and sentenced to death.

Friends of George Wilson's began circulating petitions for mercy, and public opinion was so greatly aroused that President Andrew Jackson granted him a pardon. Then, world wide news was made when the prisoner refused to accept the pardon. The government did not know how to handle the refusal of the pardon which ordinarily would mean that the man was spared and could go free.

Because the government did not know what to do, the case went to the United States Supreme Court. The Supreme Court held that the government could not honor the pardon if Wilson refused to accept it. Thus, Wilson had to hang. Chief Justice John Marshall in *United States v. Wilson*, 32 U.S. 150; 8 L. Ed. 640 (1833) wrote:

A pardon is an act of grace, proceeding from the power entrusted with the execution of the laws, which exempts the individual on whom it is bestowed from the punishment the law inflicts for a crime he has committed. It is the private, though official act of the executive magistrate, delivered to the individual for whose benefit it is intended, and not communicated officially to the court.

It is the constituent part of the judicial system, that the judge sees only with judicial eyes, and knows nothing respecting any particular case of which he is not informed judicially. A private deed, not communicated to him, whatever may be its character, whether a pardon or release, is totally unknown, and cannot be acted upon. The looseness which would be introduced into judicial proceedings would prove fatal to the great principles of justice, if the judge might notice and act upon facts not brought regularly into the cause. Such a proceeding, in ordinary cases, would subvert the best established principles, and would overturn those rules which have been settled by the wisdom of ages.

Is there any thing peculiar in a pardon which ought to distinguish it in this respect from other facts?

We know of no legal principle which will sustain such a distinction.

A pardon is a deed, to the validity of which delivery is essential; and delivery is not complete without acceptance. It may then be rejected by the person to whom it is tendered; and if it be rejected, we have discovered no power in a court to force it on him.

This is exactly like salvation in Jesus Christ. It is written, "For the wages of sin is death, but the gift of God is eternal life in Christ Jesus our Lord" (Rom. 3:23). We need the pardon in Jesus Christ, but God will not force it upon anyone.

God loves us passionately and deeply. Yet, because of our sinfulness and our constant tendency to disobey God, we are separated from Him. God is not only perfectly loving, but He is also perfectly holy and perfectly just. The holiness of God and the goodness of God require that He punish sin wherever it is found. That is why our wages are, in fact, death.

We earned damnation in hell forever because of our sinfulness. But eternal life in Christ Jesus is a gift from God. We can never earn it. And since it is a gift from God, the executive magistrate of the universe, we have to accept it for it to benefit us. If we do not accept eternal life by faith in Jesus Christ, the gift is as worthless to us as was George Wilson's pardon, which he refused to accept.

Jesus Christ is "holy, blameless, pure, set apart from sinners, exalted above the heavens" (Heb. 7:26). Several times in the Bible, God says to his people, "Be holy because I, the LORD your God, am holy" (Lev. 19:2). But what does it mean to be holy? It is to be set apart for God and pure. Purity of heart is important to God. We cannot fully understand the holiness of God in our human state. But we have ample evidence in the Bible of how overwhelming it is when a person is exposed to the fearful holiness of God.

Consider, for example, the apostle John. He wrote the Gospel of John, the three epistles from John, and, while he was in exile on the isle of Patmos, he wrote Revelation.

Remember John's special closeness to the Lord. On five occasions in the Gospel of John, he is referred to as "the disciple whom Jesus loved." John was one of the three disciples who was with Jesus when he was transfigured in glory on the mountain. At the last supper, he is the one who reclined next to Jesus. John went with Jesus into the courtyard of the high priest during Jesus' persecution before he was crucified. John was the one who stood by the cross when all the other disciples had fled. He was the one to whom Jesus entrusted his mother, Mary, after he was gone. John 19:26-27 records:

> When Jesus saw his mother there, and the disciple whom he loved standing nearby, he said to his mother, "Dear woman, here is your son," and to the disciple, "Here is your mother." From that time on, this disciple took her into his home.

Think about it! Jesus entrusted his own mother to the apostle John. If there was any man whom we might expect had a great comfort and familiarity with Jesus, it is the apostle John. What did John record when he was confronted with the glory and holiness of the resurrected Jesus in the book of Revelation? Hear what is written in Rev. 1:12-18:

> I turned around to see the voice that was speaking to me. And when I turned I saw seven golden lampstands, and among the lampstands was someone "like a son of man," dressed in a robe reaching down to his feet and with a golden sash around his chest. His head and hair were white like wool, as white as snow, and his eyes were like blazing fire. His feet were like bronze glowing in a furnace, and his voice was like the sound of rushing waters. In his right hand he held seven stars, and out of his mouth came a sharp double-edged sword. His face was like the sun shining in all its brilliance. ***When I saw him, I fell at his feet as though dead*** (emphasis mine). Then he placed his right hand on me and said: "Do not be afraid. I am the First and the Last. I am the Living

One; I was dead, and behold I am alive for ever and ever! And I hold the keys of death and Hades."

The holiness of the Lord was so overwhelming that John fell at the Lord's feet as though dead. Even the heavens are unclean in the Lord's sight (Job 15:15). In Isaiah, it is written, "All of us have become like one who is unclean, and all our righteous acts are like filthy rags" (Isa. 64:6). If our righteous acts are like filthy rags, how bad must our sinful acts look to God?

God is also perfectly just. "Righteousness and justice are the foundation of your throne; love and faithfulness go before you" (Ps. 89:14). Thus, our sinfulness towards God makes us the just objects of God's holy wrath.

Yet the grace of God is so amazing!! He loves us in spite of our wretched sinfulness. He loves us even though we deserve His wrath. There is no one who can withstand the terrible wrath of God except one. The only one who can withstand the wrath of God is God Himself. Therefore, because He loves us, He sent his son, Jesus Christ, to bear our punishment for us.

> For God so loved the world that he gave his one and only Son, that whoever believes in him shall not perish but have eternal life. For God did not send his Son into the world to condemn the world, but to save the world through him. Whoever believes in him is not condemned, but whoever does not believe stands condemned already because he has not believed in the name of God's one and only Son.
>
> John 3:16-18

And again, it is written, "Let the wicked forsake his way and the evil man his thoughts. Let him turn to the LORD, and he will have mercy on him, and to our God, for he will freely pardon" (Isa. 55:7).

III. The Other Side of the Cross - How then Shall We Live?

There are two great dangers after we have become saved. We are in continual danger of falling into error on the right hand or the left. What do I mean by this? Well, we Christians, after we have been saved, often fall into one of two camps. Either we become licentious (have loose morals) and have a lax attitude towards sin, or we become legalistic and construct a new set of rigid rules to live by, rules which squelch true grace and mercy.

In fact, different churches in the early church era (during the time of the apostle Paul) often fell into these two traps. The letters to the church in Corinth were written to a church that fell into loose morals. Paul rebuked some of the individuals severely for their lackadaisical attitude toward sin. Consider 1 Corinthians 5:1-11 (NKJV):

It is actually reported that there is sexual immorality among you, and such sexual immorality as is not even named among the Gentiles—that a man has his father's wife! And you are puffed up, and have not rather mourned, that he who has done this deed might be taken away from among you. For I indeed, as absent in body but present in spirit, have already judged (as though I were present) him who has so done this deed. In the name of our Lord Jesus Christ, when you are gathered together, along with my spirit, with the power of our Lord Jesus Christ, deliver such a one to Satan for the destruction of the flesh, that his spirit may be saved in the day of the Lord Jesus.

Your glorying is not good. Do you not know that a little leaven leavens the whole lump? Therefore purge out the old leaven, that you may be a new lump, since you truly are unleavened. For indeed Christ, our Passover, was sacrificed for us. Therefore let us keep the feast, not with old leaven, nor with the leaven of malice and wickedness, but with the unleavened bread of sincerity and truth.

I wrote to you in my epistle not to keep company with sexually immoral people. Yet I certainly did not mean with the sexually immoral people of this world, or with the covetous, or extortioners, or idolaters, since then you would need to go out of the world. But now I have written to you not to keep company with anyone named a brother, who is sexually immoral, or covetous, or an idolater, or a reviler, or a drunkard, or an extortioner—not even to eat with such a person.

Do you see how Paul had to deal with this church? Some in Corinth seemed to think, "Well, now I'm saved and Jesus paid the penalty for my sins, so I can do anything (and any sin) I want." Paul also soundly dealt with this attitude in Romans 6:8-18 (NKJV):

Now if we died with Christ, we believe that we shall also live with Him, knowing that Christ, having been raised from the dead, dies no more. Death no longer has dominion over Him. For the death that He died, He died to sin once for all; but the life that He lives, He lives to God. Likewise you also, reckon your-selves to be dead indeed to sin, but alive to God in Christ Jesus our Lord.

Therefore do not let sin reign in your mortal body, that you should obey it in its lusts. And do not present your members as instruments of unrighteousness to sin, but present yourselves to God as being alive from the dead, and your members as instruments of righteousness to God. For sin shall not have dominion over you, for you are not under law but under grace.

What then? Shall we sin because we are not under law but under grace? Certainly not! Do you not know that to whom you present yourselves slaves to obey, you are that one's slaves whom you obey, whether of sin leading to death, or of obedience leading to righteousness? But God be thanked that though you were slaves of sin, yet you obeyed from the heart that form of doctrine to which you were delivered. And having been set free from sin, you became slaves of righteousness.

Thus, we see in the Corinthian church believers who fell into immorality. In the same way today, by treating Jesus' sacrifice for us as a free ticket to sin, we do the very things that He came to save us from.

Now, consider the opposite problem: falling into legalism. Paul had to deal with that issue in the church in his letter to the Galatians. Not only the churches but the apostles themselves were not immune from falling back into Jewish legalism. Even Peter did when he separated himself from the Gentiles, people whom orthodox Jews considered unclean. Hear what Paul wrote in Galatians 2:11-13:

When Peter came to Antioch, I opposed him to his face, because he was clearly in the wrong. Before certain men came from James, he used to eat with the Gentiles. But when they arrived, he began to draw back and separate himself from the Gentiles because he was afraid of those who belonged to the circumcision group. The other Jews joined him in his hypocrisy, so that by their hypocrisy even Barnabas was led astray.

His rebuke of the whole church in Galatia for its legalism was even stronger. In Galatians 3:1-13 (NKJV), Paul wrote:

O foolish Galatians! Who has bewitched you that you should not obey the truth, before whose eyes Jesus Christ was clearly portrayed among you as crucified? This only I want to learn from you: Did you receive the Spirit by the works of the law, or by the hearing of faith? Are you so foolish? Having begun in the Spirit, are you now being made perfect by the flesh? Have you suffered so many things in vain—if indeed it was in vain?

Therefore He who supplies the Spirit to you and works miracles among you, does He do it by the works of the law, or by the hearing of faith?—just as Abraham "believed God, and it was accounted to him for righteousness." Therefore know that only those who are of faith are sons of Abraham. And the Scripture, foreseeing that God would justify the Gentiles by faith, preached the gospel to Abraham beforehand, saying, "In you all the nations shall be blessed." So then those who are of faith are blessed with believing Abraham.

For as many as are of the works of the law are under the curse; for it is written, "Cursed is everyone who does not continue in all things which are written in the book of the law, to do them." But that no one is justified by the law in the sight of God is evident, for "the just shall live by faith." Yet the law is not of faith, but "the man who does them shall live by them." Christ has redeemed us from the curse of the law, having become a curse for us (for it is written, "Cursed is everyone who hangs on a tree"), that the blessing of Abraham might come upon the Gentiles in Christ Jesus, that we might receive the promise of the Spirit through faith.

The Galatian church had forgotten the primary purpose of the law. In Galatians 3:24-25, we read, "So the law was put in charge to lead us to Christ that we might be justified by faith. Now that faith has come, we are no longer under the supervision of the law."

Once we believe in Jesus Christ, the law of God has served its purpose. Jesus came not to abolish the law, but to fulfill it and fulfill all of its dreadful requirements. In Romans 8:1-4, it is written:

Therefore, there is now no condemnation for those who are in Christ Jesus, because through Christ Jesus the law of the Spirit of life set me free from the law of sin and death. For what the law was powerless to do in that it was weakened by the sinful nature, God did by sending his own Son in the likeness of sinful man to be a sin offering. And so he condemned sin in sinful man, in order that the righteous requirements of the law might be fully met in us, who do not live according to the sinful nature but according to the Spirit.

The law's purpose is to drive us into the arms of our savior, Jesus Christ. We cry out, "Lord, have mercy on me, a sinner!" and we are saved by faith in Jesus Christ who paid the just penalty for our sin.

So, bearing that in mind, let us serve the Lord with incredible gratitude, not ignoring God's standards for righteousness and thereby showing contempt for the blood of Jesus Christ. Let us also not fall under the spell of legalism where we lose sight of the freedom and joy we have as children of God who are loved by God.

Our life in the Lord is based on love. "If ye love Me, ye will keep My commandments" John 14:15 (R.V.). Consider what Chambers said in *My Utmost for His Highest* in the devotional for November 2nd:

> Our Lord never insists upon obedience; He tells us very emphatically what we ought to do, but He never takes means to make us do it. We have to obey Him out of a oneness of spirit. That is why whenever Our Lord talked about discipleship, He prefaced it with an IF - you do not need to unless you like. "*If* any man will be My disciple, let him deny himself," let him give up his right to himself to Me. Our Lord is not talking of eternal positions, but of being of value to Himself in this order of things, that is why He sounds so stern (cf. Luke 14:26). Never interpret these words apart from the One Who uttered them.

> The Lord does not give me rules, He makes His standard very clear, and if my relationship to Him is that of love, I will do what He says without any hesitation. If I hesitate, it is because I love some one else in competition with Him, viz., myself. Jesus Christ will not help me to obey Him, I must obey Him; and when I do obey Him, I fulfill my spiritual destiny. My personal life may be crowded with small petty incidents, altogether unnoticeable and mean; but if

I obey Jesus Christ in the haphazard circumstances, they become pinholes through which I see the face of God, and when I stand face to face with God I will discover that through my obedience thousands were blessed. When once God's Redemption comes to the point of obedience in a human soul, it always creates. If I obey Jesus Christ, the Redemption of God will rush through me to other lives, because behind the deed of obedience is the Reality of Almighty God.[27]

In conclusion, let's hold fast to that most important truth that Jesus said when, in the garden of Gethsemane before His crucifixion, when He was praying for Himself, His disciples, and for us: "Now this is eternal life: that they may know you, the only true God, and Jesus Christ, whom you have sent" (John 17:3).

CHAPTER 5

The Divine Romance

Presented by Rick Davis January 25, 2005

to the TAX Chapter at the Estelle Unit, Huntsville, Texas.[28]

—⟋⟍⟋—

I. The Current Social and Political Landscape

F riends, today we are going to look at the spiritual imagery in marriage. Our country was founded primarily by men and women who feared God and believed that the Bible is true. Their beliefs shaped our Constitution and laws. Let us look briefly at the law's roots in marriage.

Long ago, in *Maynard v. Hill*, 125 U.S. 190 (1888), the U.S. Supreme Court characterized marriage as "the most important relation in life," (*id.* at 205) and as "the foundation of the family and of society, without which there would be neither civilization nor progress" (*id.* at 211). In *Meyer v. Nebraska*, 262 U.S. 390 (1923), the court recognized that the right "to marry, establish a home and bring up children" is a central part of the liberty protected by the Due Process Clause (*id.* at 399). In *Skinner v. Oklahoma ex rel. Williamson*, 316 U.S. 535, 541 (1942), the court said "marriage and procreation are fundamental to the very existence and survival of the race."

The institution of marriage is and has been under attack in this country. More than half of all marriages end in divorce, often leaving ruined lives, mountains of debt, and permanently scarred children in their wake. Many in this country want to redefine marriage to include a union between two persons of the same sex.

Sadly, the rate of divorce among professing Christians is about the same as that of the rest of society.[29] We have become a nation that looks out for number one, and we always find a way to justify our selfishness. Jesus told us, "Love your neighbor as yourself." He never told us and, indeed, never had to tell us to love ourselves. We do that already to the extreme. It is our self-indulgent prideful sinfulness that separates us from God.

Yet, there are still many people in this country who steadfastly hold to the sanctity of marriage and are dedicated to defending it. Many still regard it as holy. Most significantly, God says that marriage is important and holy. The Bible says, "Marriage should be honored by all, and the marriage bed kept pure, for God will judge the adulterer and all the sexually immoral" (Heb. 13:4).

II. The Holiness of God

Before we take an in-depth view of what the Bible says about marriage, we should consider God and his holiness. God loves us passionately and deeply. Yet because of our sinfulness, our constant tendency to disobey God, we are separated from Him. God does not only perfectly love, but He is also perfectly holy and perfectly just. The holiness of God and the goodness of God require that He punish sin wherever it is found.

Jesus Christ is "holy, blameless, pure, set apart from sinners, exalted above the heavens" (Heb. 7:26). Several times in the Bible, God says to his people, "Be holy because I, the LORD your God, am holy" (Lev. 19:2). But what does it mean to be holy? It is to be set apart for God and pure.

Purity of heart is important to God. We cannot fully understand the holiness of God in our human state. We have ample evidence in the Bible, however, of how overwhelming it is when a person is exposed to the fearful holiness of God.

Consider, for example, the apostle John. He wrote the Gospel of John, the three epistles from John, and, while he was in exile on the isle of Patmos, he wrote Revelation. Think about John's special closeness to the Lord. On five occasions the Gospel of John refers to him as "the disciple whom Jesus loved." John was one of the three disciples with Jesus when he was transfigured in glory on the mountain. At the last supper, he is the one who reclined next to Jesus.

John went with Jesus into the courtyard of the high priest during Jesus' persecution before he was crucified. John was the one who stood by the cross when all the other disciples had fled. He was the one to whom Jesus entrusted his mother, Mary, after he was gone.

Yet in Revelation 1:12-18, when John was confronted with the risen Lord, the sight was so overwhelming that he fell at the Lord's feet as though dead. Even the heavens are unclean in the Lord's sight (Job 15:15). In Isaiah, it is written, "All of us have become like one who is unclean, and all our righteous acts are like filthy rags" (Isa. 64:6). If our righteous acts are like filthy rags, how bad must our sinful acts look to God?

God is also perfectly just. "Righteousness and justice are the foundation of your throne; love and faithfulness go before you" (Ps. 89:14). Our sinfulness towards God makes us the just objects of God's holy wrath.

Yet the grace of God is so amazing!! He loves us in spite of our wretched sinfulness. He loves us even though we deserve His wrath. There is no one who can rise again after being smitten by the terrible wrath of God except one. That one is Jesus Christ, and it is by the power of God that He is risen.

"We love because he first loved us" (1 John 4:19). Because God first loved us, we can love Him. The great author C.S. Lewis wrote:

> The event of falling in love... In one high bound it has overleaped the massive wall of our selfhood; it has made appetite itself altruistic, tossed personal happiness aside as a triviality and planted the interests of another in the centre of our being.[30]

Thus God, by loving us even when we were wretched, sinful, rebellious, and unlovable, makes us able to love Him. And He enables us to put His interests in the center of our being. God longs to be longed for. King David, the man after God's own heart, longed for God with passion. In the Psalms, he wrote, "As the deer pants for streams of water, so my soul pants for you, O God" (Ps. 42:1).

III. God's Human Picture

God gives us human relationships to teach us about Himself, His love for us, and how He longs to be loved by us. The Ten Commandments first appear in Exodus 20. After that, God sets forth various laws.

Interestingly, the first set of laws God gave to the Hebrews had to do with the treatment of servants. A Hebrew was to set free another Hebrew slave after seven years. But if a Hebrew servant had been given a wife by whom he later had children, and if, at the time he was to be set free, "the servant declares, 'I love my master and my wife and children and do not want to go free,' then his master must take him before the judges. He shall take him to the door or the doorpost and pierce his ear with an awl. Then he will be his servant for life" (Ex. 21:5-6).

The Bible tells us, "Taste and see that the LORD is good; blessed is the man who takes refuge in him." (Ps. 34:8). Jesus tells us, "My yoke is easy and my burden is light" (Mt. 11:30). God wants us to know that, in serving Him there is both true joy and true freedom.

But God goes further and gives us children to help us understand how much He loves us as His children. As Moses told the Israelites before they entered the Promised Land, "The LORD your God, who is going before you, will fight for you, as he did for you in Egypt, before your very eyes, and in the desert. There you saw how the LORD your God carried you, as a father carries his son, all the way you went until you reached this place" (Deut. 1:30-31).

But God goes even further still to teach us about Him and gives us the most holy of institutions ordained among mankind, the institution of marriage. In the book of Hosea, God spoke of a day where He says, "You will call me 'my husband'; you will no longer call me 'my master'" (Hos. 2:16). Again, in Isaiah it is written, "For your Maker is your husband— the LORD Almighty is his name—the Holy One of Israel is your Redeemer; he is called the God of all the earth" (Isa. 54:5).

God teaches us through the symbolism in marriage about His deep love for us and how He longs for us to love Him. The Song of Solomon is a book of love and of passion. It describes the relationship between King Solomon and his bride, the Shulamite.

The book is also a picture of Jesus Christ and His love for His bride, the church. In Song of Solomon 4:12, we read, "A garden enclosed is my sister, my spouse, a spring shut up, a fountain sealed." Consider how that godly Chinese evangelist, Watchman Nee, contemplated this passage:

> To live a life in the depths, it is necessary to have direct and intimate communion with the Lord. What is spoken of here is a garden. As seen in the Bible, a garden is God's very first thought. Unlike ordinary land for general purpose planting, or a field specifically for tillage, a garden is solely for the object of beauty and visual enjoyment. In a garden there may be trees but the object is not for the wood; or fruit trees but the purpose is still not for the bearing of fruit. The importance of a garden is attached to its flowers. They are planted only for their beauty. To plant flowers is therefore for pleasantness to the eyes. To describe this garden as an "inclosed garden" is to mean that it is not a public park to which everybody may have access for seeking enjoyment but is inclosed exclusively for Christ and His glory. The beauty within is to be seen and appreciated by Christ alone. This in-depth life is not meant to please men but Christ only.
>
> This kind of life is "a spring shut up." A spring is for people to use; though it is so, it is still reserved for the pleasure of the Lord.
>
> This sort of life is "a fountain sealed." A spring is brought into being by human labor but a fountain is not. A spring is of men but a fountain is of God. A fountain stands for the joy and contentment we acquire in the presence of God. Such experience is not to be deliberately disclosed to other people because it is a sealed fountain.

In a word, a Christian should not intentionally exhibit his beauty, pursuit and spiritual experience for people to see. On the other hand, everything of his in-depth experience should be silently sealed up for the Lord. Only this kind of life in the depths will satisfy the Lord's heart.

Brothers and sisters, our life is often too shallow and too large a proportion of it is exposed on the surface. May God show us grace by permitting the Cross to do deeper work within us so that we may strike roots in order to have life in the depths to fulfill God's requirements and satisfy His heart.[31]

It is a sad but true fact that many young men and women treat their bodies like public parks instead of enclosed gardens. God did not intend for us to be that way. Indeed, some people treat their bodies like train stations for all to pass through with no thought of their future spouses or how precious sexual intimacy with that future person is intended to be.

Virginity, that is sexual purity before marriage, is important to God, especially in its symbolism. In describing Rebekah, the woman who was to be Isaac's bride, we read, "The girl was very beautiful, a virgin; no man had ever lain with her" (Gen. 24:16). It was required of the high priest in Old Testament times that "the woman he marries must be a virgin" (Lev. 21:13).

If an Israelite man falsely accused his new bride of not having been a virgin, the man was punished for giving an "Israelite virgin a bad name" (Deut. 22:19). If his allegations were true, however, then she was stoned to death for having "done a disgraceful thing in Israel by being promiscuous while still in her father's house" (Deut. 22:21). In fact, sexual intimacy was treated as so unique that a man who violated a woman by raping her was put to death.

But if out in the country a man happens to meet a girl pledged to be married and rapes her, only the man who has done this shall die. Do nothing to the girl; she has committed no sin deserving death. This case is like that of someone who attacks and murders his neighbor, for the man found the girl out in the country, and though the betrothed girl screamed, there was no one to rescue her.
Deuteronomy 22:25-27

Because rape is such a deeply hurtful crime, God's law puts it on the same rung as murder. Rape is symbolic of Satan violating, exploiting, and tormenting our souls. This is why a forced conversion is never pleasing to God. God is not a rapist. Satan is. God is more forbearing and more self restrained than the most noble-minded gentleman ever was. God waits for His tender, virtuous, and beautiful bride to yield to Him.

Just as our relationship with God as His believers is deeply intimate, God wants our devotion to our spouses to be exclusive and deeply intimate. God calls us to be holy because He is holy. What, then, can we say is God's passionate desire? Jesus Christ desires a wife, a faithfully devoted and virtuous yet erotically passionate wife. And we who believe are the Bride of Christ.

IV. Divorce

The Bible is clear in its expression of God's will about marriage. Let us digress for a moment and talk about the failed marriage. The Bible is just as clear about how God feels about divorce. Consider this passage from the book of Malachi:

You weep and wail because he no longer pays attention to your offerings or accepts them with pleasure from your hands. You ask, "Why?" It is because the LORD is acting as the witness between you and the wife of your youth, because you have broken faith with her, though she is your partner, the wife of your marriage covenant.

Has not the LORD made them one? In flesh and spirit they are his. And why one? Because he was seeking godly offspring. So guard yourself in your spirit, and do not break faith with the wife of your youth.

"I hate divorce," says the LORD God of Israel, "and I hate a man's covering himself with violence as well as with his garment," says the LORD Almighty. So guard yourself in your spirit, and do not break faith.
Malachi 2:13-16

God intended marriage to last a lifetime: until death do us part. Yet the Lord gives us a marriage to Himself that lasts forever. "After that, we who are still alive and are left will be caught up together with them in the clouds to meet the Lord in the air. And so we will be with the Lord forever" (1 Thess. 4:17).

V. The Garments Required for God's Bride

What sort of bride does God require for His Son, Jesus Christ? Do you remember what we saw in Leviticus? It was required of the high priest in Old Testament times that "the woman he marries must be a virgin" (Lev. 21:13). God requires that same virtuousness of the bride for His Son, and her virtuousness is in her garments.

In Matthew 22:1-14 (NKJV) we read:

And Jesus answered and spoke to them again by parables and said: "The kingdom of heaven is like a certain king who arranged a marriage for his son, and sent out his servants to call those who were invited to the wedding; and they were not willing to come. Again, he sent out other servants, saying, 'Tell those who are invited, "See, I have prepared my dinner; my oxen and fatted cattle are killed, and all things are ready. Come to the wedding."' But they made light of it and went their ways, one to his own farm, another to his business. And the rest seized his servants, treated them spitefully, and killed them. But when the king heard about it, he was furious. And he sent out his armies, destroyed those murderers, and burned up their city. Then he said to his servants, "The wedding is ready, but those who were invited were not worthy. Therefore go into the highways, and as many as you find, invite to the wedding." So those servants went out into the highways and gathered together all whom they found, both bad and good. And the wedding hall was filled with guests.

But when the king came in to see the guests, he saw a man there who did not have on a wedding garment. So he said to him, 'Friend, how did you come in here without a wedding garment?' And he was speechless. Then the king said to the servants, "Bind him hand and foot, take him away, and cast him into outer darkness; there will be weeping and gnashing of teeth." For many are called, but few are chosen.

This parable refers to the kingdom of heaven. Jesus said so. Some parts of it are also easy to understand. The king is God. The son is Jesus Christ. Those who were invited initially represent the Jews who did not fear God and did not have faith in God.

Those who seized the king's servants and abused them and killed them represent the evil men and women who persecuted the true prophets and messengers of God in days of old. The ordinary people who were brought in off the streets, the commoners, the ruffians, the rapscallions like all of us, represent the Gentiles (that is, non-Jews) who are invited to believe.

An Aside

Now let me say as an aside, we who are believers should never be arrogant towards or resentful of the Jew. They are God's chosen people, and He desires their reconciliation to Himself. The apostle Paul very clearly explains this in Romans 9-11. If you know someone who is a Messianic Jew (that is, a Jew who has become a believer), then bless him. If you know a Jew who has not yet become a believer, then bless him anyway. For the Jew is evidence of God's faithfulness and enduring purpose throughout the ages. He has a plan to redeem the Jewish people through the Messiah just as he does for us Gentiles. God said in Isaiah 49:6:

> *It is too small a thing for you to be my servant to restore the tribes of Jacob and bring back those of Israel I have kept. I will also make you a light for the Gentiles, that you may bring my salvation to the ends of the earth.*

Let's get back to the parable. For years, I could not understand the meaning of that part of the parable having to do with the man who was not wearing wedding clothes being cast into hell. It seemed so harsh, so cruel. After all, he seemed like one of those ordinary guys who were simply brought in off the street. Why should he be held responsible if he was not wearing wedding clothes? How could he have known he was going to a wedding when he dressed that morning?

I wondered about this passage for years after I became a Christian, and I did not understand it until recently. In the meantime, I, like a multitude of men and women throughout history, basically sat in judgment of God, thinking that he was harsh and arbitrary in this part of the parable.

The key to this parable is in what the garments represent. They represent the righteousness of Christ. As is written in Isaiah 61:10, "I delight greatly in the LORD; my soul rejoices in my God. For he has clothed me with *garments of salvation* and arrayed me in a *robe of righteousness*, as a bridegroom adorns his head like a priest, and as a bride adorns herself with her jewels" (emphasis added).

Paul wrote two passionate letters to the church in Corinth. He loved those people like his own children, his own little flock. It is because of this garment of salvation and robe of righteousness that God gives to the believer that Paul could tell the Corinthians, "I am jealous for you with a godly jealousy. I promised you to one husband, to Christ, so that I might present you as a pure virgin to him" (2 Cor. 11:2).

Also read what Paul wrote to the church in Galatia in Galatians 3:26:

You are all sons of God through faith in Christ Jesus, for all of you who were baptized into Christ have *clothed yourselves with Christ.* There is neither Jew nor Greek, slave nor free, male nor female, for you are all one in Christ Jesus. If you belong to Christ, then you are Abraham's seed, and heirs according to the promise (emphasis added).

Do you see, my friends, that when we believe in Jesus Christ, He takes away all of our sin, not part, but all, and makes us pure. He makes us, His people, His church as a whole, the pure, virgin bride of Jesus Christ.

Jesus Christ is perfectly righteous, and His righteousness is imputed to us. It is freely given to us. It does not come from within ourselves; it is given to us by God. As it is written, "For it is by grace you have been saved, through faith—and this not from yourselves, it is the gift of God— not by works, so that no one can boast" (Eph. 2:8-9). Praise God that salvation does not depend at all on us. All we do is believe and accept His incredible gift.

VI. The Profound Mystery

In marriage, the intimate relationship between a husband and wife is as if the two have their souls poured into the same cup and are mingled. The church is the bride of Christ. Just as we are in Christ, Christ is in us. Our bodies are the temple of the Holy Spirit.

The Song of Solomon is, and I mean no irreverence in saying this, the most erotic and passionate book of the Bible. It is a book about the indescribable bliss of a husband's and a wife's intimate relationship.

The only time God speaks to the couple is in chapter five where he tells them, "Eat, O friends, and drink; drink your fill, O lovers" (Song of Sol. 5:1). This book is a profound picture of the love between husband and wife, and it reveals that God wants husbands and wives to enjoy the passion of their intimacy.

God does not want his people to be His lackeys. He does not want us to be as slaves who cower in the presence of a terrible, angry master. God wants a loving bride, a bride who is passionate and faithfully devoted to Him.

Just as God opened the side of Adam to create woman, the side of Jesus Christ was opened on the cross. The shedding of blood is for the redemption of His people, and the water that flowed out of the Lord's side symbolizes the Holy Spirit. Just as Adam and his bride became one flesh, Jesus Christ and His bride become one Spirit.

Out of Christ's side, God is creating a bride for Himself. That bride is the priesthood of believers. Do you remember our discussion about Solomon and his bride, the Shulamite? The Hebrew word for Shulamite is simply the feminine form of the word for Solomon. The late Witness Lee, one of Watchman Nee's co-laborers, said it well:

> With the rib which was taken out of Adam, God built a woman as Adam's counterpart (Gen. 2:22-24). The rib taken out of Adam signifies the flowing water and unbroken bone mentioned in John 19:34 and 36. When Christ died on the cross, His side was pierced and the water of life came out, strong as an unbreakable bone, to produce the church as His counterpart. Thus, the sinner whom God created and who became fallen, after being redeemed and transformed by Christ's death and resurrection, becomes the woman in the universe to be married to Christ.[32]

Jesus appeared to Paul (formerly Saul) and commissioned him to tell the world about the love of Jesus Christ and God's longing desire for us to be reconciled to Him. Paul wrote the Ephesians about how the marriage of a husband and wife is a picture of God's passionate love for his people, the bride of Christ. Hear what Paul wrote to the Ephesians:

> Wives, submit to your own husbands, as to the Lord. For the husband is head of the wife, as also Christ is head of the church; and He is the Savior of the body.

Therefore, just as the church is subject to Christ, so let the wives be to their own husbands in everything.

Husbands, love your wives, just as Christ also loved the church and gave Himself for her, that He might sanctify and cleanse her with the washing of water by the word, that He might present her to Himself a glorious church, not having spot or wrinkle or any such thing, but that she should be holy and without blemish. So husbands ought to love their own wives as their own bodies; he who loves his wife loves himself. For no one ever hated his own flesh, but nourishes and cherishes it, just as the Lord does the church. For we are members of His body, of His flesh and of His bones. "For this reason a man shall leave his father and mother and be joined to his wife, and the two shall become one flesh." This is a great mystery, but I speak concerning Christ and the church. Nevertheless let each one of you in particular so love his own wife as himself, and let the wife see that she respects her husband.

Ephesians 5:22-33

The language in verse 22 about wives submitting to their husbands is repugnant to most of secular society. The unbelieving world sees this verse as a tool to make women servile, and, to the Lord's anguish, throughout the centuries many evil men have used the verse for just that purpose.

This verse is offensive to so many because the world almost never sees a husband loving his wife as Christ loves the church: sacrificially. How many husbands would freely lay down their lives for their wives? How many husbands would take delight in washing their wives' feet? How infrequently do we see the husband who will take a stand to oppose the whole world for his wife, though she was fallen and had a past more checkered than Mary Magdalene?

Jesus adores His bride, the church, is jealous for her, and desires her affection and intimacy far more fervently than the most ardent of grooms on his wedding night.

Paul calls the uniting of husband and wife into one flesh a profound mystery. Yet "he who unites himself with the Lord is one with him in spirit" (1 Cor. 6:17). The Lord is "intimate with the upright" (Prov. 3:32 NASB).

One of the most revealing things that Jesus ever said was in John 17. The passage is known as the high priestly prayer which the Lord prayed in the Garden of Gethsemane shortly before He was crucified. In John 17:3, the Lord prayed, "Now this is eternal life: that they may know you, the only true God, and Jesus Christ, whom you have sent."

The Greek word translated "know" here is *ginosko*. It means intimate knowledge, and we see that truth from another New Testament passage in Matthew 1:24-25. After Joseph woke up from the dream where the Lord appeared to him and told him not to be afraid to take Mary for his wife, it is written, "When Joseph woke up, he did what the angel of the Lord had commanded him and took Mary home as his wife. But he had no union with her until she gave birth to a son. And he gave him the name Jesus."

The Greek word that is translated "union with" in these verses and which clearly refers to Joseph's sexual relations with Mary is the same *ginosko*. Eternal life is knowing God and Jesus Christ with a depth of intimacy far greater than that in the sexual relationship between a husband and a wife.

One of the seven angels who had the seven bowls full of the seven last plagues came and said to me, "Come, I will show you the bride, the wife of the Lamb." And he carried me away in the Spirit to a mountain great and high, and showed me the Holy

City, Jerusalem, coming down out of heaven from God. It shone with the glory of God, and its brilliance was like that of a very precious jewel, like a jasper, clear as crystal.

Revelation 21:9-11

God is creating a bride for Jesus Christ, a wife to be co-regent with Him forever. Though the world scoffs at a reverent, holy view of marriage, God intends our marriages on earth to be a picture of the eternal relationship between Jesus Christ and His bride, the church.

May God bless the reading and study of His Word. May he make us passionately devoted to Him. As for us, let us be like David, a man after God's own heart.

CHAPTER 6

The Parable of the Four Soils

Presented by Rick Davis January 29, 2006
during Chapel service at the Estelle Unit, Huntsville, Texas.

—m—

I. Foundations

Friends, before we begin the primary message, I want
to introduce myself. I know many of you, but there are
some of you whom I have not had the privilege of meeting.
At the outset, I want to say that I was a sinner in need of a
Savior just like some of you still are.

I am no better than any of you. Those of you who already
know me have heard me quote Oswald Chambers, that great
missionary to the English and Australian troops during World
War I. He was a committed servant of the Lord and is one
of my favorites. He is best known for his work *My Utmost
for His Highest*, the world's most popular devotional. In the
devotional for June 1st, Chambers wrote:

> When God wants to show you what human nature
> is like apart from Himself, He has to show it you in
> yourself. If the Spirit of God has given you a vision
> of what you are apart from the grace of God (and He

only does it when His Spirit is at work), you know there is no criminal who is half so bad in actuality as you know yourself to be in possibility. My "grave" has been opened by God and "I know that in me (that is, in my flesh) dwelleth no good thing." God's Spirit continually reveals what human nature is like apart from His grace.[33]

Chambers was exactly right. Do you see what this means men? God sees my thought life. No matter what any of you have done to get yourselves here, no matter how bad the crime, I know in my heart of hearts that I am no better than any of you. I was a vile sinner in desperate need of a Savior.

Thus, when you hear this message, don't think of me as a district judge. I am one spiritual beggar telling another where to find bread. My fervent hope and prayer is that this message blesses you, and that you receive it in the spirit that it is given. That is, receive it from one who has been humbled by God and broken by His law.

II. The Parable's Importance and the Meaning of the Seed and the Four Soils

Jesus told his disciples many parables to explain to them the way of salvation and the kingdom of God. The parable of the sower of the seed on four soils is one of the most important parables Jesus told. Jesus Christ Himself said, "Don't you understand this parable? How then will you understand any parable?" (Mark 4:13).

This parable appears in three different Gospels, Matthew, Mark, and Luke. On each occasion, Jesus gave an explanation of the parable.

In order to understand the parable of the sower, we must understand what the seed signifies and what the soil signifies. Jesus used seeds in other parables in different ways.

Here, the seed represents the Word of God. The type of soil represents a man's heart and the way his heart receives the Word. Let's look at Mark's rendition of the parable closely:

> He taught them many things by parables, and in his teaching said: "Listen! A farmer went out to sow his seed. As he was scattering the seed, some fell along the path, and the birds came and ate it up. Some fell on rocky places, where it did not have much soil. It sprang up quickly, because the soil was shallow. But when the sun came up, the plants were scorched, and they withered because they had no root. Other seed fell among thorns, which grew up and choked the plants, so that they did not bear grain. Still other seed fell on good soil. It came up, grew and produced a crop, multiplying thirty, sixty, or even a hundred times."

> Then Jesus said, "He who has ears to hear, let him hear."

> When he was alone, the Twelve and the others around him asked him about the parables. He told them, "The secret of the kingdom of God has been given to you. But to those on the outside everything is said in parables so that,

>> "they may be ever seeing but never perceiving, and ever hearing but never understanding; otherwise they might turn and be forgiven!""

> Then Jesus said to them, "Don't you understand this parable? How then will you understand any parable? The farmer sows the word. Some people are like seed along the path, where the word is sown. As soon as they hear it, Satan comes and takes away

the word that was sown in them. Others, like seed sown on rocky places, hear the word and at once receive it with joy. But since they have no root, they last only a short time. When trouble or persecution comes because of the word, they quickly fall away. Still others, like seed sown among thorns, hear the word; but the worries of this life, the deceitfulness of wealth and the desires for other things come in and choke the word, making it unfruitful. Others, like seed sown on good soil, hear the word, accept it, and produce a crop—thirty, sixty or even a hundred times what was sown.

Mark 4:2-20

It is in Mark's account that Jesus Christ Himself tells us that this parable is critical and its understanding gives us insight into other parables in the Gospels. The last of the three accounts appears in the Gospel of Luke. In Luke 8:11 we see that the seed in this parable represents the Word of God.

III. The First Soil - Those Hostile to the Gospel

The seed that fell along the path and was trampled and eaten by birds represents those to whom the gospel is presented but who never believe. Birds are often used in the Bible as symbolic of Satan or of evil. When God invoked the Abrahamic covenant in Genesis 15, He commanded Abraham to make a sacrifice of animals cut in half. After waiting on God for a long time, Abraham had to drive birds of prey away from the carcasses. The birds were trying to devour the sacrifice.

Similarly, in Genesis 40 we read that one of Pharaoh's servants, the chief baker, had a dream while in prison. He dreamed that he had three baskets on his head, and birds were eating bread out of the top basket. When the baker's fellow inmate, Joseph son of Jacob, interpreted the dream, he told the baker that the baker would be hung on a tree after his head was cut off, and birds would eat his flesh.

Likewise, when the Lord comes as a conqueror riding a white horse into battle, an angel standing in the sun will call to all the birds flying in mid-air to "Come, gather together for the great supper of God, so that you may eat the flesh of kings, generals, and mighty men, of horses and their riders, and the flesh of all people, free and slave, small and great" (Rev. 19:17b-18).

The seed that falls on the path and which is eaten by birds represents those who never believe in Jesus. Satan "takes away the word from their hearts, so that they may not believe and be saved" (Luke 8:12).

There are people in this world who truly scoff when you tell them about Jesus Christ. They mock the gospel and the Bible. They have no interest in God and no care for the coming judgment.

The gospel message makes no sense to people represented by the seed scattered along the path. As Paul says in 1 Corinthians 2:18, "For the message of the cross is foolishness to those who are perishing, but to us who are being saved it is the power of God." He says further in 1 Corinthians 2:14, "The man without the Spirit does not accept the things that come from the Spirit of God, for they are foolishness to him, and he cannot understand them, because they are spiritually discerned."

In fact, some of you here today may feel this way and may not understand why you even showed up this morning. Lord willing, He will make all things clear to you this morning, including the way to be saved. Even our ability to understand spiritual things is a gift from God.

IV. The Fourth Soil - The Great Fruit Bearers

We've talked about the seed strewn on the path and what it means. That's an easy one. Likewise, not much needs to be said about understanding the meaning of the seed that is sown in good soil because this obviously refers to the committed believers whose faith is evident by what they do.

In John 14:13-14, Jesus spoke of the people in whose heart the gospel takes root and bears fruit, that is, those who have faith in Him. There, the Lord said: "I tell you the truth, anyone who has faith in me will do what I have been doing. He will do even greater things than these, because I am going to the Father. And I will do whatever you ask in my name, so that the Son may bring glory to the Father. You may ask me for anything in my name, and I will do it."

The Lord also said in John 15:16, "You did not choose me, but I chose you and appointed you to go and bear fruit— fruit that will last. Then the Father will give you whatever you ask in my name." For the believer represented as seed being sown on good soil, his enduring fruit is obvious.

V. The Hard to Understand Part - The Second and Third Soils - and Two Competing Theories

We have addressed the first and the fourth soils. These two are easy to understand. The second and third soil types are not so easily understood.

A. One Theory

Some think that the seed on rocky soil, the seed in the thorny patch of ground, and the seed sown on good soil are all three different types of believers. The fourth type represents productive, God-honoring men and women who are faithful in their walk, but the second and third soils simply represent backslidden believers. Under this interpretation, the middle two soils represent people who followed the Lord at one time, then fell back into a life of sin.

In their view, the second, third, and fourth seeds all represent believers because the seed germinated in each case. They think that each person became a new creation just as Jesus used the germination of a seed to illustrate saving faith: "Unless a kernel of wheat falls to the ground and dies, it remains only a single seed. But if it dies, it produces many seeds" (John 12:24).

The error in this line of reasoning is the manner in which the seed is viewed. True, Jesus at times used the germination of a seed to illustrate death to self followed by new life or new birth, but in the parable of the sower of the four soils the seed is the Word of God, not various types of men's hearts. It is the differences in the soils in our parable which represent various types of men's hearts.

B. Another Theory

While some say that only the first soil represents the unsaved while the other three are saved, others argue that only the fourth type of soil represents the saved person. They reason that unless a man has totally surrendered his life to the Lord, he is not really saved, and thus, the second and third soils represent false converts.

This belief is sometimes called "lordship theology." Its proponents would quote John the Baptist, who in Matthew 3:8 warned that we should "produce fruit in keeping with repentance," and they would argue that the absence of continual fruit is evidence of the absence of true salvation.

We all know of a person who accepted Jesus in the past, repented of his godless living, and, after a time, fell back into a selfish, greedy, lustful way of living. When confronted with such a person, those who adhere to this second school of thought rationalize their view by saying, "Well, that person did not really believe in the first place." Not only is this pat answer presumptuous and intellectually arrogant, it also ignores the scriptural truth that some backslidden but true believers will enter heaven as those barely escaping the flames. The apostle Paul described such a man in 1 Corinthians 13:10-15:

> By the grace God has given me, I laid a foundation as an expert builder, and someone else is building on it. But each one should be careful how he builds. For no one can lay any foundation other than the one already laid, which is Jesus Christ. If any man builds on this foundation using gold, silver, costly stones, wood, hay or straw, his work will be shown for what it is, because the Day will bring it to light. It will be revealed with fire, and the fire will test the quality of each man's work. If what he has built survives, he will receive his reward. If it is burned up, he will suffer loss; he himself will be saved, but only as *one escaping through the flames* (emphasis added).

Believing in Jesus Christ unto salvation does not exempt us from sin in this lifetime. In fact, we are certain to sin again. The Bible is clear about that (1 John 1:8-10).

Paul, in Romans 7:14-25, candidly and honestly acknowledges the civil war against sin that raged within him until he learned how he had to die daily to his self life and continually yield to the Lord every day.

To conclude that the second and third soils can only represent those who were false converts, people who say they belong to Jesus but really do not, does not take into account what we know from the Bible about indwelling sin within the believer.

VI. An Aside - Security of Genuine Salvation

At this point, it is quite natural for us to wonder, "Could one or both of these two middle soils represent someone who believed in Jesus at one point, then turned away from the faith, and is now damned?"

Consider what Paul wrote in Ephesians: "For it is by grace you have been saved, through faith—and this not from yourselves, it is the gift of God—not by works, so that no one can boast" (Eph. 2:8-9). If even the faith we have that reconciles us to God is, itself, a gift from God, then we can take credit for nothing.

God calls us to repent of our sins and accept the free gift of eternal life through faith in Jesus Christ. Through this faith, we freely accept God's sacrifice as the payment of the debt for our own sins. Through this faith in Christ which God has given us, we are spared from our just punishment, which was eternity in hell.

If we are saved and have faith in Jesus Christ, it is only because God gave us the gift of faith in the first place. And if we have salvation, we have no reason to be proud of ourselves; it is totally from God. We also know that "He [Jesus] is able to save completely those who come to God through him, because he always lives to intercede for them" (Heb. 7:25).

Finally, we see in Romans 11:29 that "God's gifts and his call are irrevocable." Once God has you, He is not going to let you go. Our salvation, once we have it, does not depend on us continuing to do good.

VII. The Second Soil - The Stony Ground Hearer a.k.a. the False Convert

It is possible for one to think that he can get salvation and forgiveness without repentance. Some people think of Jesus as a free ticket to heaven, and they continue to sin to the brim in this lifetime. In the book of Jude 1:3-5, it is written:

> Dear friends, although I was very eager to write to you about the salvation we share, I felt I had to write and urge you to contend for the faith that was once for all entrusted to the saints. For certain men whose condemnation was written about long ago have secretly slipped in among you. They are godless men, who change the grace of our God into a *license for immorality* and deny Jesus Christ our only Sovereign and Lord.

> Though you already know all this, I want to remind you that the Lord delivered his people out of Egypt, but later destroyed those who did not believe (emphasis added).

From this passage in Jude, we see that there are some who intellectually acknowledge that Jesus Christ paid the price for sin, but they seek forgiveness without repentance. True salvation, or genuineness in conversion, involves death toward sin and a recognition that we are hopeless to stand before God unless we have relief provided by God. If we treat Jesus' sacrifice as simply a license to sin, we deny the very thing from which Jesus saved us, that is, the penalty of sin and the power of sin.

Consider the exodus of the Israelites out of slavery in Egypt, and then consider their imminent entry into the Promised Land. God allowed those who did not believe the promises of God about the Promised Land to die in the desert, and He raised up a new generation of Israelites.

Because the men and women who entered the Promised Land were children when the law of God was first given through Moses, God commanded Moses to give the law a second time in Deuteronomy to renew the covenant. Consider what God said of one who viewed the promise of God as a license to sin as set forth in Deuteronomy 29:17-21:

> You yourselves know how we lived in Egypt and how we passed through the countries on the way here. You saw among them their detestable images and idols of wood and stone, of silver and gold. Make sure there is no man or woman, clan or tribe among you today whose heart turns away from the LORD our God to go and worship the gods of those nations; make sure there is no root among you that produces such bitter poison.
>
> When such a person hears the words of this oath, he invokes a blessing on himself and therefore thinks, "I will be safe, even though I persist in going my own way." This will bring disaster on the watered land as well as the dry. The LORD will never be willing to forgive him; his wrath and zeal will burn against that man. All the curses written in this book will fall upon him, and the LORD will blot out his name from under heaven. The LORD will single him out from all the tribes of Israel for disaster, according to all the curses of the covenant written in this Book of the Law.

It is an horrific thing to be one whom the Lord would "never be willing to forgive." This is the one who approaches the sacrifice of Jesus Christ lightly and views His death and atoning sacrifice as simply a license to sin. In light of these truths, now consider the three accounts of the seed that fell on rocky soil, first looking at Matthew 13:5 and Mark 4:5:

> Some fell on rocky places, where it did not have much soil. It sprang up quickly, because the soil was

shallow. But when the sun came up, the plants were scorched, and they withered because they had no root.

Let's also consider Jesus' explanation in Mark 4:17 of the seed sown in rocky soil:

Others, like seed sown on rocky places, hear the word and at once receive it with joy. But since they have no root, they last only a short time. When trouble or persecution comes because of the word, they quickly fall away.

The Word of God cannot take root in such a man's life because of the hardness of the soil, that is, the hardness of his heart. "The Lord detests all the proud of heart. Be sure of this: They will not go unpunished" (Prov. 16:5). "God opposes the proud but gives grace to the humble" (James 4:6).

When a proud man is ridiculed because of professed faith in Jesus, he is embarrassed because he cares more about the approval of his fellow man that the approval of God. Because God opposes the proud but gives grace to the humble, God cannot remain true to His Word and give His grace to the proud of heart.

Therefore, the "stony ground" hearer is the one who hears the word, but seeks forgiveness without repentance. He may even think that it sounds like a really good deal – heaven for the taking. In all three accounts of this parable, Jesus says that these people "hear the word, and receive it with joy."

He shows no contrition and does not have that "broken and contrite heart" (Ps. 51:17). He may even think that he is doing God a favor. He does not recognize that he is a sinner in need of a Savior, one who has seriously offended God and is deserving of eternal damnation. Although the gospel sounds really good to such a man, he thinks in his heart that he does not really need Jesus.

This is the one who is described in Hebrews 6:4-6 and 10:26-31. Such a man never was saved, though he professed to be so. He may have even appeared to be a believer. Instead, he hears the word and sees it simply as an opportunity to be blessed by God. He treats Jesus Christ as if he were simply fire insurance from the pits of hell.

VIII. The Third Soil - The Thorny Soil Hearer a.k.a. the Worldly or Backslidden Christian

Unlike the faithful, fruitful Christian who sins from time to time and has the knowledge of his need for a life of continued brokenness before God, the backslidden Christian is one who has become ensnared by the cares and temptations of this world, has become miserable, and has become spiritually unfruitful. Consider the seed that fell among thorns in all three accounts:

Other seed fell among thorns, which grew up and choked the plants. (Matt. 13:7)

Other seed fell among thorns, which grew up and choked the plants, so that they did not bear grain. (Mark 4:7)

Other seed fell among thorns, which grew up with it and choked the plants. (Luke 8:7)

In all three accounts of the third soil, the plant was choked. From Luke's account, we know that the plant grew with the thorns. A plant cannot grow up unless it takes root in soil.

Thus, the Word of God took root in this person's heart. The soil of the man's heart was not so stony that it could not take root. But the plant was also choked. The plant did not die, but it was so sapped of vital energy that it bore no grain according to Mark's account. Now consider Jesus' explanation of the seed among thorns.

The one who received the seed that fell among the thorns is the man who hears the word, but the worries of this life and the deceitfulness of wealth choke it, making it unfruitful. (Matt. 13:22)

Still others, like seed sown among thorns, hear the word; but the worries of this life, the deceitfulness of wealth and the desires for other things come in and choke the word, making it unfruitful. (Mark 4:18-19)

The seed that fell among thorns stands for those who hear, but as they go on their way they are choked by life's worries, riches and pleasures, and they do not mature. (Luke 8:14)

Jesus describes the plant as being unfruitful and immature. The things that choke this believer are the worries of this life, the deceitfulness of wealth, desires for riches, and pleasures.

The believer Paul described in 1 Corinthians 3, who enters heaven as one barely escaping the fire, is the believer who has become unfruitful and who never matured because of the cares of this world. Thus, the backslidden but genuine believer is represented by the soil plagued with thorns, the third of the four soils.

IX. Conclusion of the Parable of the Four Soils

In conclusion, we see the following. The first seed scattered on the path is never a believer and has no interest in God or the coming judgment.

The second seed sown on rocky ground is one who professes to be a believer, but because of the hardness of his heart never truly believes unto salvation. This is the false convert of whom the Lord spoke in Matthew 7:21-23:

> Not everyone who says to me, 'Lord, Lord,' will enter the kingdom of heaven, but only he who does the will of my Father who is in heaven. Many will say to me on that day, 'Lord, Lord, did we not prophesy in your name, and in your name drive out demons and perform many miracles?' Then I will tell them plainly, 'I never knew you. Away from me, you evildoers!'

The third seed sown among thorns is one who truly believes but becomes ensnared and tangled in sin and by the cares and troubles of this world. One might not even recognize him as a believer. He becomes unfruitful, but he is saved entering heaven as one barely escaping the flames.

Finally, the fourth seed sown in good soil is the believer who, with a noble heart, repents of his sin and recognizes that, because of his sins, he was an abomination to the Lord. With deep, abiding gratitude he accepts the gift of salvation through Jesus Christ and yields to the Lord and lives for Him.

One thing we must always remember is that we cannot see the soil. Only God can see the heart (Psalm 44:21 and Acts 15:8). The stony ground hearer who is a false convert may look as godly (or even more so) as the solidly committed believer represented by the seed sown in good soil.

Similarly, the backslidden but true believer who has become choked by the things of this world may look as godless as the one represented by the seed strewn on the path. At times, the stony ground hearer will look just like the thorny patch believer. These are things we mortals cannot judge. Only God can judge the heart.

X. The Way to Be Saved

Regrettably, some preachers make the way of salvation harder to understand than it really is. God does not want us to mouth coldly and heartlessly some "sinner's prayer." He does not call us to feel like we need a Savior, and salvation does not depend on whether we feel sorry enough for our sins. We may not want to give up our self-indulgent sinning. We may not even want to be saved. We do not even have to fully understand what Jesus did for us on the cross in order for God to begin His saving work.

God is concerned with our hearts. Think about all the examples in the Bible that bear this out. When the thief on the cross said, "Jesus, remember me when you come into your kingdom," did the Lord stop him and say, "Do you repent of your sins?" No, "Jesus answered him, 'I tell you the truth, today you will be with me in paradise'" (Luke 23:42-43).

When a woman who had been subject to bleeding for twelve years touched the Lord and Jesus confronted her, the Bible says that "the woman, seeing that she could not go unnoticed, came trembling and fell at his feet. In the presence of all the people, she told why she had touched him and how she had been instantly healed." After that, did Jesus say, "Do you understand your need for repentance or remission of sins?" No, the Word says that Jesus "said to her, 'Daughter, your faith has healed you. Go in peace'" (Luke 8:47-48).

When the Roman centurion anguished over his servant who was paralyzed and lay suffering, he asked the Lord for help. Jesus said that He would come and heal him.

> The centurion replied, "Lord, I do not deserve to have you come under my roof. But just say the word, and my servant will be healed. For I myself am a man under authority, with soldiers under me. I tell this one, 'Go,' and he goes; and that one, 'Come,' and he comes. I say to my servant, 'Do this,' and he does it." When Jesus heard this, he was astonished and said to those following him, "I tell you the truth, I have not found anyone in Israel with such great faith.
>
> Matthew 8:8-10

What each one of us needs is an encounter with almighty God with an honest heart. Watchman Nee, a great evangelist from China, put the matter about as clearly as I have ever seen it when he set out four guiding principles:

> God has made, from His side, a threefold provision for every man in his hour of crisis. First, Jesus has come as the Friend of sinners; second, it is He personally (and no intermediary) whom men are called to meet; and third, the Holy Spirit has been poured out upon all flesh, to bring to pass in man the initial work of conviction of sin, repentance and faith, and of course, all that follows. Then, finally, from the side of the sinner, one condition and only one is demanded. He is not required - in the first place - to believe, or to repent, or to be conscious of sin, or even to know that Christ died. He is required only to approach the Lord with an honest heart.[34]

Remember that God opposes the proud, but He gives grace to the humble. Humble yourself in the sight of the Lord, and He will lift you up. Be honest with God. Come to the Lord in humility and unburden your heart before Him. May God bless this study of His Word.

CHAPTER 7

The Lord's Hatred of Racism; the Lord's Love of Brotherhood

Presented by Rick Davis May 30, 2006
to the TAX Chapter at the Estelle Unit, Huntsville, Texas.

—ᄴᄼ—

I. Our Nation's Laws and Constitution

I love my country. I thank God that I live in this country. For all its faults that the media persistently reports about it, I think that this is the best place to be. Over the centuries, we have had some great, noble-minded leaders. One of my favorite people, in fact, one of my heroes, is Abraham Lincoln. As you know, he was President of the United States during and after the Civil War until he was assassinated. He is best known for the Emancipation Proclamation, a presidential order that freed the slaves in all of the states in rebellion. Lincoln was moved to do this as fulfillment of a promise to God.

On July 10, 1858, as part of the Lincoln-Douglas debates, Lincoln said in a speech the following:

My friend has said to me that I am a poor hand to quote Scripture. I will try it again, however. It is said in one of the admonitions of the Lord, 'As your Father in Heaven is perfect, be ye also perfect.' The Savior, I suppose, did not expect that any human creature could be perfect as the Father in Heaven.... He set that up as a standard, and he who did most toward reaching that standard, attained the highest degree of moral perfection. So I say in relation to the principle that all men are created equal, let it be as nearly reached as we can. If we cannot give freedom to every creature, let us do nothing that will impose slavery upon any other creature.

At a speech given at Lewistown, Illinois on August 17, 1858, Lincoln criticized the ethical neutralism of his opponent, Stephen Douglas. Lincoln referred specifically to slavery in a speech that was an appeal to the deeper meaning of the Declaration of Independence and to the original thirteen colonies. Hear what Lincoln said:

These communities, by their representatives in old Independence Hall, said to the whole world of men: "We hold these truths to be self evident: that all men are created equal; that they are endowed by their Creator with certain unalienable rights; that among these are life, liberty and the pursuit of happiness." This was their majestic interpretation of the economy of the Universe. This was their lofty and wise and noble understanding of the justice of the Creator to His creatures. Yes, gentlemen, to *all* His creatures, to the whole great family of man. In their enlightened belief, nothing stamped with the Divine image and likeness was sent into the world to be trodden on, and degraded, and imbruted by its fellows. They grasped not only the whole race of man then living, but they reached forward and seized upon the farthest posterity. They erected a beacon to guide their children and their children's children, and the countless myriads who should inhabit the earth in other ages.

Lincoln firmly believed that the dignity of man is derivative. That is to say that Lincoln did not see man as good in and of himself. He saw that man derives his own glory from being created in the image of the living God.

Abraham Lincoln loved God and feared God. He also revered the Constitution and took his oath of office very seriously. Many people have forgotten that the Emancipation Proclamation only applied to the slaves in the rebel states. He knew that he had the authority to declare their freedom in states that were in rebellion and where martial law could be said to exist (even though the Union certainly did not control much of the territory in the South when the proclamation was issued).

But Lincoln also knew that he did not have the authority, under the Constitution, to free slaves that may be present in what were usually free states. He knew that a constitutional amendment abolishing slavery could (and would) come later, but he did what he could lawfully do during the time of war. His proclamation was not all that was needed, but it was a strong move in the right direction.

In his second letter to the Corinthians, the apostle Paul said, "Finally, brothers, good-by. Aim for perfection, listen to my appeal, be of one mind, live in peace. And the God of love and peace will be with you" (2 Cor. 13:11). Abraham Lincoln exhorted Americans to aim for the very things that Paul said that the Corinthian Christians should.

So have we, as a nation, reached that highest degree of moral perfection of which Lincoln spoke as it relates to respecting our fellows regardless of race? Obviously, we have not. Yet, if we love God, we ought to continue to seek that end. For it is an expression of love for God and to our fellow man when we truly act like we believe that all men were created equal, and we love each other without regard to race, parentage, or skin color.

II. The Holy Law of God

Now, we know that the United States Constitution and the Texas Constitution define and protect our rights. We know also that all of our federal and state laws protect our rights and govern our conduct, oftentimes by telling us what is against the law to do.

All of us have violated the law in some respect, some in bigger ways, some in smaller ways. Some have only committed traffic violations; some people have committed very serious, very cruel crimes. But if a person violates the law, is sentenced after conviction, and then serves the complete sentence, does the law have any further hold on the man? No, no additional punishment can be assessed for that previous violation of the law.

But the law of God is altogether different from man's law. Granted, it does tell us things that we should not do. Yet, all of us at some point have violated God's law, some in bigger ways, and some in smaller ways. Can any one of us say that we have fully paid the penalty for even one of our violations of God's holy law?

If we are honest with ourselves, we have to admit that we have not and that we cannot. The Bible says that the eyes of God are too pure even to look upon evil. Thus, if we are to stand before God and have fellowship with Him, we have to be made pure.

This brings us to the purpose of God's law. God's law is not so much to provide us with a checklist of things to do. Instead, God's law makes us painfully and dreadfully aware of our need for a Savior. The apostle Paul tells us in Romans 7:13, "The law is holy, and the commandment is holy, righteous and good." But we also see in Psalm 19:7, "The law of the LORD is perfect, reviving the soul."

That's from the NIV. The NKJV translates the verse: "The law of the LORD is perfect, converting the soul." What is it that revives or converts the soul? Why, Scripture is very clear: it is the law of the Lord.

John Bunyan, the author of that Christian classic *Pilgrim's Progress*, said, "The man who does not know the nature of the Law cannot know the nature of sin." Likewise, Martin Luther said, "The first duty of the gospel preacher is to declare God's Law and show the nature of sin."[35]

John Wesley said "The first use of [the Law], without question, is to convince the world of sin. By this is the sinner discovered to himself. All his fig-leaves are torn away, and he sees that he is 'wretched and poor and miserable, blind and naked.' The Law flashes conviction on every side. He feels himself a mere sinner. He has nothing to pay. His 'mouth is stopped' and he stands 'guilty before God.'"[36]

Much of modern Christianity and many churches have forgotten this powerful and necessary truth. Jesus is often preached as the great life enhancer. "Give your heart to Jesus, and He will give you love, joy, peace, and happiness... He will heal your drinking problem, your drug problem, your marital problem, your problem with anger" and so forth. To be sure, faith in Jesus Christ changes us from the inside out, but we have to come to Jesus in humility with a humble heart.

With the law of God, God breaks the hard heart. With the gospel, God heals the broken heart. Friends, if I examine myself and you examine yourself in the light of the Ten Commandments, you and I can see that we deserve hell. We deserve God's eternal punishment.

The holiness of God is so great that His justice requires sin to be punished wherever it is found. Because the justice of God is so thorough, so complete, so overwhelming, so dreadful, we see that we are in desperate need of the mercy of God. And how is it that we obtain the mercy of God? We obtain it by faith in Jesus Christ. The law was given to make us aware of our need for a Savior and to show us what we would do if we truly loved God.

III. The Greatest Commandment

Now let us consider the passage in Matthew when Jesus was asked the greatest commandment in the law.

> "Teacher, which is the greatest commandment in the Law?" Jesus replied: "'Love the Lord your God with all your heart and with all your soul and with all your mind.' This is the first and greatest commandment. And the second is like it: 'Love your neighbor as yourself.' All the Law and the Prophets hang on these two commandments."
>
> Matthew 22:37-40

What is it that God really wants? God wants us to love Him and to love our fellow man. He wants us to love Him more passionately than any lover.

From Genesis to Revelation, the Bible is about God's creating a bride for Himself out of mankind. Think about it. When God created woman, he put Adam into a deep sleep. Then God opened his side and took out a rib and created woman. The woman is the counterpart to man. In the same way, the church is the counterpart to Jesus Christ.

The Bible is one great love story. The most erotic book in the Bible is the Song of Solomon. Solomon's bride is the Shulamite woman. Do you realize that the Hebrew word Shulamite is simply the feminine version of the Hebrew word for Solomon?

God is preparing us, that is, we believers, to be the bride of Christ. Just as God opened the side of Adam to create woman for man, God opened the side of Jesus Christ when he hung on the cross. Out of Jesus' side flowed blood and water: blood for the redemption from sin and judgment, water to symbolize the life-giving Holy Spirit. Everything that happens to us happens to fulfill God's purpose in our lives and to perfect us as His bride.

Do you see how the law of God not only makes us aware of our need for a Savior, but also shows us what our actions would be like if we truly loved God and our neighbor? It teaches the nature and intent of the second greatest commandment.

If I love my neighbor, I will not pursue his wife in any kind of improper relationship. If I love him, I will want to strengthen his relationship with his wife, and my actions towards him will further that. If I love God, I will not even think improper thoughts about his wife because that would dishonor God and reveal that I am also discontent with the life that God has provided for me. It would be as if I were saying, "God, your love is not enough for me."

If I love my neighbor, I will not steal his possessions. Usually, his possessions represent his or his family member's hard work. If I, indirectly, am forcing one to work to replace what I have stolen, I have put that person into a form of slavery. If I love God, then I will not even covet (or earnestly desire) my neighbor's possessions.

If I love my neighbor, I will not lie to him because lies are the tools of the enemy, Satan. Lies also offend our heavenly Father, for God is Spirit and his worshipers must worship him in Spirit and in truth. Jesus even said, "I am the way, and the truth, and the life. No one comes to the father except through me" (John 14:6).

If I love my God, I will honor my parents, because I know that this pleases God. I will love my earthly parents even if they are not worthy of love because they did not provide for me, they abandoned me, or they abused me. Instead, I will love them with the compassion of God with the fervent hope that they may come to repentance, repenting of the sins that they may have done, and with the fervent hope that they would come to saving faith in Jesus Christ.

If I love God, I will not take His name in vain, for His name is above all names and He is worthy of all power, honor, glory, and majesty. Also, if I love my neighbor, I will not take God's name in vain, because I don't want to lead my neighbor to disrespect God or lack a desire to love God.

If I love God, I will not put anyone or anything before Him: not my wife, not my children, not my possessions, nothing. For if I love God, I will recognize that every good and perfect gift is from above, and even the hardships that I endure come with the permission of my loving Father, that He may draw me closer to Himself.

There is none but Christ. Jesus Christ is the beginning and the end, and is the magnificent expression of God's sacrificial love for us.

IV. The Lord's Hatred of Racism

Let us move on to the primary message. God hates racism. We can see this clearly in His Word. The Bible is clear that God is not a respecter of persons. He does not show favoritism. During the formation of the early church, and after it was revealed to Peter that the gospel of Jesus Christ is for the Gentiles (non-Jews) as well as the Jews, Peter said in Acts 10:34-35, "I now realize how true it is that God does not show favoritism but accepts men from every nation who fear him and do what is right." (The King James Version renders this sentence "God is not a respecter of persons.")

Second, Paul wrote, "There is neither Jew nor Greek, slave nor free, male nor female, for you are all one in Christ Jesus. If you belong to Christ, then you are Abraham's seed, and heirs according to the promise" (Gal. 3:28-29). Thus, in the eyes of God, it makes no difference if a believer is a man or woman, black, white, Hispanic, Asian, or any other race. We who believe in Jesus Christ are all one in Him.

The Bible is also very clear that Jesus will come a second time to the earth. The first time he came as a suffering servant. The second time he will come as a conquering king. Terrible times will come upon the earth before Jesus' second coming (2 Tim. 3:1-5), and things will go from bad to worse as the time draws nearer. When describing the times shortly before His return, Jesus said in Matthew 24:4-8:

> Watch out that no one deceives you. For many will come in my name, claiming, `I am the Christ,' and will deceive many. You will hear of wars and rumors of wars, but see to it that you are not alarmed. Such things must happen, but the end is still to come. Nation will rise against nation, and kingdom against kingdom. There will be famines and earthquakes in various places. All these are the beginning of birth pains.

The Greek word in this passage that is translated "nation" is *ethnos*. Ethnos could also be accurately translated as "ethnic group." I bring this verse to your attention to show you that Jesus lists ethnic group rising up against ethnic group among all of the bad things coming upon the earth. The Lord lists racism as a bad thing.

For an even more vivid and powerful Biblical illustration of God's attitude towards racism, we should go back to the Old Testament. Remember that Miriam was Moses' sister, and Aaron was their brother. Remember also that Moses was very close to God: "The LORD would speak to Moses face to face, as a man speaks with his friend" (Ex. 33:11).

There came a time when Miriam instigated grumbling against her brother Moses, apparently resenting his position, and she led Aaron to do the same. They used the fact that

Moses had married an Ethiopian woman as an excuse for criticism (some Bible translations use the phrase "Cushite woman" but it is generally accepted that Cush is what is now known as Ethiopia). The account is found in Numbers 12:1-3 (NKJV):

> Then Miriam and Aaron spoke against Moses because of the Ethiopian woman whom he had married; for he had married an Ethiopian woman. So they asked "Has the LORD indeed spoken only through Moses? Has He not spoken through us also?" And the LORD heard it. (Now Moses was very humble, more than all men who were on the face of the earth.)

God summoned Miriam and Aaron to appear before Him. He rebuked them and, apparently because Miriam was the chief instigator, God afflicted her with leprosy. In Numbers 12:10-13 it is written: "When the cloud lifted from above the Tent, there stood Miriam—leprous, like snow. Aaron turned toward her and saw that she had leprosy; and he said to Moses, 'Please, my lord, do not hold against us the sin we have so foolishly committed. Do not let her be like a still-born infant coming from its mother's womb with its flesh half eaten away.' Moses cried out to the LORD, 'O God, please heal her!'"

From this passage, we see that Moses had married a woman whose skin was probably very black. It is easily and reasonably inferred that God has no problem with interracial marriages. Thus, we should not have any problem with them either. God punished Miriam for speaking against both Moses' authority and Moses' Ethiopian wife.

But the nature of Miriam's punishment reveals even more than that. In order to understand the significance of the nature of Miriam's punishment, it is useful to look at another circumstance immediately preceding this one to see how God sometimes dealt with those who grumbled against Him.

Consider when the Israelites wandered in the desert and grumbled against God and craved meat.

> The rabble with them began to crave other food, and again the Israelites started wailing and said, "If only we had meat to eat! We remember the fish we ate in Egypt at no cost—also the cucumbers, melons, leeks, onions and garlic. But now we have lost our appetite; we never see anything but this manna!"
>
> Numbers 11:4-6

In Numbers 11:18-20 Moses said, "Consecrate yourselves in preparation for tomorrow, when you will eat meat. The LORD heard you when you wailed, 'If only we had meat to eat! We were better off in Egypt!' Now the LORD will give you meat, and you will eat it. You will not eat it for just one day, or two days, or five, ten or twenty days, but for a whole month—until it comes out of your nostrils and you loathe it—because you have rejected the LORD, who is among you, and have wailed before him, saying, 'Why did we ever leave Egypt?'"

How God dealt with the grumbling Israelites and gave them what they asked for is set forth in Numbers 11:31-34:

> Now a wind went out from the LORD and drove quail in from the sea. It brought them down all around the camp to about three feet above the ground, as far as a day's walk in any direction. All that day and night and all the next day the people went out and gathered quail. No one gathered less than ten homers. Then they spread them out all around the camp. But while the meat was still between their teeth and before it could be consumed, the anger of the LORD burned

against the people, and he struck them with a severe plague. Therefore the place was named Kibroth Hattaavah, because there they buried the people who had craved other food.

Men, do you see the significance of the nature of God's punishment? When the people complained about not having anything but manna, God said, in essence, "You want meat? I will give you so much meat that you will be repulsed by it; it will come out of your noses."

Now look how God rebuked Miriam in light of this passage that immediately precedes the account of Miriam's grumbling against Moses and his Ethiopian wife. Miriam resented Moses and used his interracial marriage as a pretext to criticize him and stir up trouble against him. She appealed to the peoples' inner, ungodly prejudices and looked down on Moses' wife because she was darker in appearance.

Miriam was presumably light skinned in appearance. As her punishment, God made her leprous, white as snow. It is as if God were saying to her, "You think you are so special because you are white? I will make you white as snow, and your flesh will appear hideous, half eaten away."

There were only three other occasions in the Bible where a person was afflicted with leprosy as a form of discipline. They were Gehazi, Elisha's servant (2 Kings 5:27), King Azariah (2 Kings 15:5), and King Uzziah (2 Chron. 26:19). In all three of these other cases, the men showed contempt for the holiness and grace of God. Miriam's case was the first and was intended to be a warning (Deut. 24:9).

Whenever we look down on other people because of the color of their skin, we are being contemptuous of God, His holiness, and His image. They are created in the image of God just like the rest of us. Thus, from a biblical perspective, not only is racism a bad thing, God hates racism.

We could end the discussion here with this conclusion that God hates racism. But if we want to pursue personal godliness, we should go further and examine Moses' response. Remember we serve Him who said, "It is mine to avenge; I will repay" (Deut. 32:35), and Moses apparently had that attitude as well.

Few things are more hurtful to a person than to see a spouse ridiculed, mocked, or despised. Indeed, for most people, for one to see his or her spouse hurt is worse then suffering the wound oneself.

Surely Moses ached when he heard insults hurled at his wife. Yet how did he respond? He responded with godly compassion, recognizing that Miriam's and Aaron's foolishness provoked the wrath of God. When he saw Miriam's punishment, "Moses cried out to the LORD, 'O God, please heal her!'" (Num. 12:13).

When we are targets of racism—whether racism forward or racism in reverse— we ought to have compassion for the foolish. As our Lord said at the Sermon on the Mount, "Love your enemies and pray for those who persecute you, that you may be sons of your Father in heaven" (Matt. 5:44).

V. The Lord's Love of Brotherhood

When God hates something, He usually loves its opposite. Knowing that God hates racism, can we tell that God loves brotherhood and men expressing brotherly love towards one another? From His Word we can see that the answer is clearly, "Yes."

In Psalm 133:1, it is written, "How good and pleasant it is when brothers live together in unity!"

To the Ephesians, Paul wrote, "Peace to the brothers, and love with faith from God the Father and the Lord Jesus Christ. Grace to all who love our Lord Jesus Christ with an undying love" (Eph. 6:23-24). And without drawing any distinction between men or women or the nationality of the people at Colossae, Paul wrote, "To the holy and faithful brothers in Christ at Colossae: Grace and peace to you from God our Father" (Col. 1:2).

God called Peter to lead a Gentile (non-Jew) named Cornelius to the Lord. Jews ordinarily did not associate with Gentiles. Peter had a dream recounted in Acts 10 where he saw unclean animals and was told by the Lord to kill and eat. He protested and said that he had never eaten anything unclean. The Lord told him, "Do not call anything impure that God has made clean" (Acts 10:15). When he finally arrived at Cornelius' house, Peter said, "I now realize how true it is that God does not show favoritism but accepts men from every nation who fear him and do what is right" (Acts 10:34-35).

Finally, in the last chapter of the Bible, Revelation 22:1-2, it is written:

> Then the angel showed me the river of the water of life, as clear as crystal, flowing from the throne of God and of the Lamb down the middle of the great street of the city. On each side of the river stood the tree of life, bearing twelve crops of fruit, yielding its fruit every month. And the leaves of the tree are for the healing of the nations.

Again, the Greek word translated "nations" is *ethnos*, meaning ethnic groups. In the eternal kingdom, God will heal all of the pain throughout all of history brought about by racism.

Men, I encourage and exhort you: let's have a little heaven on earth. Let us love our fellow man without regard to race, parentage, or skin color. May God bless you, and may God bring great revival to the Estelle Unit.

CHAPTER 8

Spiritual Warfare and the Serpent's Covenant

by Judge Rick Davis September 19, 2006
to TAX Chapter at the Estelle Unit, Huntsville, Texas.

—⟋⟋⟋—

I. The Basics

Friends, before I begin with our primary text, I want to review the basics with you. I have known many of you for some time. Some of you are deep in the faith and have been walking with the Lord for a long time. For some of you, this may be our first time together. So I want to make sure that we are all on the same footing.

First of all, do you know the difference between the law of God and the grace of God, and do you know the purpose of each? I'll start with the Ten Commandments, for those are the most important elements of God's law.

God's law says that we shall not steal. How many of you have ever stolen something, even if just once? The value of the item is not important. God's law tells us not to lie. How many of you have ever told a lie? God's law prohibits adultery. How many of you have committed adultery? Before you answer that, remember that God considers a lustful thought for a woman not your wife the same as doing the deed.

How many of you have committed murder? Again, before you raise your hand, remember God considers an unjustified hateful thought towards another or harsh word said to another to be the same as committing murder. You see, men, if we are honest with ourselves, we are all lying, thieving, adulterous murderers at heart, and we have only looked at four of the Ten Commandments.

As it is written in Romans 3:19-20, "Now we know that whatever the law says, it says to those who are under the law, so that every mouth may be silenced and the whole world held accountable to God. Therefore, no one will be declared righteous in his sight by observing the law; rather, through the law we become conscious of sin." Psalm 19:7 reads: "The law of the LORD is perfect, reviving the soul." Thus, we see throughout Scripture that the law of God revives or awakens our consciences. It makes us aware of God's holy and righteous requirements.

What are the consequences of our chronic sinfulness? In Romans 6:23, it is written, "For the wages of sin is death." We know also from the Bible that the eyes of God are too pure to look upon evil (Hab. 1:13). Sinful man cannot stand in the presence of the most holy God.

Men, what does violation of God's law mean we deserve? We deserve hell. Righteousness and justice are the foundation of God's throne (Psalm 89:14). The perfect justice of God and the perfect holiness of God require that God punish sin wherever it is found. Thus, although the law revives our conscience, it also slays us at the same time (2 Cor. 3:6). It makes us aware not only of God's holy requirements, but also of our hopelessness in trying to meet them. The law thus also makes us aware of our desperate need for a Savior.

Earlier, I cited the first half of Romans 6:23. The grace of God is revealed in the second half of that verse: "but the gift of God is eternal life." Do you see that we earn death by our sinfulness? We cannot earn salvation, however, no matter how good we try to be. For it is written, "All our righteous acts are like filthy rags." (Isa. 64:6). Salvation is a gift from God. God gives us Himself to save us. In 1 Tim. 2:5-6, it is written, "For there is one God and one mediator between God and men, the man Christ Jesus, who gave himself as a ransom for all men—the testimony given in its proper time."

In John 5:24, Jesus Christ said, "I tell you the truth, whoever hears my word and believes him who sent me has eternal life and will not be condemned; he has crossed over from death to life." And as Paul wrote in Romans 10:8-10, "'The word is near you; it is in your mouth and in your heart,' that is, the word of faith we are proclaiming: That if you confess with your mouth, 'Jesus is Lord,' and believe in your heart that God raised him from the dead, you will be saved. For it is with your heart that you believe and are justified, and it is with your mouth that you confess and are saved."

Therefore, men, if you are one of those here today who has not yet received Jesus, get out from under the curse of the law today. Confess with your mouth that Jesus is Lord, and believe in your heart that God raised him from the dead. Let today be your spiritual birthday, the day that you are born again, born of the Spirit (John 3:5-6). If today is the day you believe, make it concrete by sharing it with Chaplain Salmon or a friend.

II. Some Background about Old Testament Symbolism

During this message today, we will talk about some symbolism in the Old Testament. If you are a new believer or have been a believer for a while but do not know the Bible very well, I encourage you to spend time in the Word daily. Read it, learn it, and meditate upon it. I guarantee you that you will be blessed. If you have never read the Bible before, you should, yet be patient with yourself. It took me more than two years to read it cover to cover the first time.

Before you plunge into reading Genesis to Revelation, you may want to learn some of the more essential truths and concepts. If a brand-new Christian were to ask me where to start reading the Bible, I would say to read the Gospel of John, the book of Genesis, then the book of Romans. Repeat that cycle a few times before taking on the whole Bible.

In the Gospel of John, you will see the love of God and the compassion of Jesus Christ portrayed quite clearly. In Genesis, you will learn many foundational truths, and you need to know Genesis to understand many important Bible truths explained in the New Testament. For example, in the book of Galatians, Paul uses Abraham's child born of Hagar to illustrate the law and Abraham's child born of Sarah to illustrate God's grace. In a similar way, in that same book, Paul uses Abraham's life story to show that we are saved by believing God, not by any works. God credits that faith as righteousness.

Yet, in the book of James, the writer rebukes those who say that they have faith but do nothing at all to show it (that is, they have no deeds consistent with their profession of faith). In order to do this, he uses Abraham's story to show that true faith is proven by the actions that follow faith. How could one begin to understand either of these two analogies unless he understood something about Abraham's life revealed in Genesis?

There are many other examples of Old Testament symbolism that foreshadowed things to come; some even foreshadowed Jesus Christ. Consider, for example, Joseph, son of Jacob. He was the first born of Jacob's favorite wife, Rachel. Jesus is the first born of many sons of God. Joseph was despised by his brothers and cast into a pit. Jesus was despised by his brothers, the Jews, crucified, and then He descended into the pits of hell. Joseph was raised to a position of glory, second only to Pharaoh. Jesus was resurrected and sits at the right hand of God. Joseph took a Gentile bride. Jesus took a Gentile bride, the church. There are many more parallels Joseph's life story.

Finally, after reading Genesis, I would suggest you read Romans. The book of Romans is the most comprehensive book in the Bible, and it explains basic Christian doctrine from beginning to end. It has been called the most important letter and the most important book in the history of the world. Read these three books a few times, and then tackle the whole Bible.

Let's move on, though, and talk about how some of these Old Testament symbols reveal the nature of spiritual warfare and what Satan intends to do to us.

III. Our Enemy, Satan, and his *M.O.* (Modus Operandi)

Any experienced warrior will tell you that it is important to understand your enemy. Satan is our enemy. Think about the first words that he ever said to mankind. Go back to Genesis 3 when the serpent tempted Eve. The serpent said to her, "Did God really say?" (Gen. 3:1).

Satan has been saying that ever since. He wants us to doubt God's truthfulness. Satan takes great delight when he sees people mock the Word of God or express doubts about its truth. When that happens, he has won a victory and deceived another soul.

The Bible says of itself that "all Scripture is God-breathed" (2 Tim. 3:16), and that it is the Word of truth (John 17:17, Eph. 1:13, and Jas. 1:18). Psalm 138:2 says that God has exalted his name and his Word above all things. From the very beginning, Satan, that ancient serpent, has sought to make us disbelieve God's word. Jesus said of Satan, "When he lies, he speaks his native language, for he is a liar and the father of lies" (John 8:44b). Thus, first and foremost, Satan is the consummate liar, and one of his primary weapons against us is to make us doubt the Word of God.

Satan is also the accuser who maligns us and defames us before God. Revelation 12:10 reads, "Then I heard a loud voice in heaven say: 'Now have come the salvation and the power and the kingdom of our God, and the authority of his Christ. For the accuser of our brothers, who accuses them before our God day and night, has been hurled down.'" That is a direct reference to Satan's fall. Zechariah 3 provides another example of Satan's evil accusing work. Consider this passage from Zechariah 3:1-2:

> Then he showed me Joshua the high priest standing before the angel of the LORD, and Satan standing at his right side to accuse him. The LORD said to Satan, "The LORD rebuke you, Satan! The LORD, who has chosen Jerusalem, rebuke you! Is not this man a burning stick snatched from the fire?"

Likewise, in the book of Job, before the heavenly host "the LORD said to Satan, 'Have you considered my servant Job? There is no one on earth like him; he is blameless and upright, a man who fears God and shuns evil'" (Job 1:8). Satan, again, always the accuser, said, "Does Job fear God for nothing? Have you not put a hedge around him and his household and everything he has? You have blessed the work of his hands, so that his flocks and herds are spread throughout the land. But stretch out your hand and strike everything he has, and he will surely curse you to your face" (Job 1:9-11). Satan smeared Job's integrity before God. Thus, a second important fact about Satan is that he is the accuser who always seeks to tear us down before God.

Satan also seeks to devour us. In the book of Job, when God asked Satan where he had come from, "Satan answered the LORD, 'From roaming through the earth and going back and forth in it'" (Job 1:6). In 1 Peter 5:8, it is written, "Your enemy the devil prowls around like a roaring lion looking for someone to devour." Thus, the third fact that we see is that Satan seeks to devour us.

Satan is also a deceiver and a masquerader. This fact is tied in with the first fact we observed, but we need to understand how he deceives. The apostle Paul, when writing the Corinthians about men who had infiltrated among them to undermine their faith, wrote, "For such men are false apostles, deceitful workmen, masquerading as apostles of Christ. And no wonder, for Satan himself masquerades as an angel of light. It is not surprising, then, if his servants masquerade as servants of righteousness. Their end will be what their actions deserve" (2 Cor. 11:13-15).

This concept is very important to know and understand. Satan deceives us by appearing good. There are many false converts in this world. On three occasions, Paul mentions that he was wounded by false brethren. If even an apostle like Paul can be deceived by false converts, how much more can we ordinary men be deceived by people controlled by Satan who appear to everyone to be servants of righteousness?

Jesus warned us, "For false Christs and false prophets will appear and perform great signs and miracles to deceive even the elect—if that were possible" (Matt. 24:24). Throughout Scripture we see that things will get far worse before the second coming of the Lord. In 2 Thessalonians 2:9-10, Paul warns us that "the coming of the lawless one will be in accordance with the work of Satan displayed in all kinds of counterfeit miracles, signs and wonders, and in every sort of evil that deceives those who are perishing. They perish because they refused to love the truth and so be saved."

This is why it is important to test every teaching against the Scriptures as the Bereans did in Acts 17. We should also test the spirits. As it is written in 1 John 4:1-3:

Dear friends, do not believe every spirit, but test the spirits to see whether they are from God, because many false prophets have gone out into the world. This is how you can recognize the Spirit of God: Every spirit that acknowledges that Jesus Christ has come in the flesh is from God, but every spirit that does not acknowledge Jesus is not from God.

An important fourth fact to learn is that Satan is a fraud.

Thus, just by examining these few verses, we see that Satan is a liar. Satan is our accuser. Satan is a destroyer who seeks to devour us. Satan is a masquerader and a deceiver. Satan is a counterfeit. In short, Satan hates us with a fiery passion, and he is our enemy.

We should not fear him, but we should respect his power. Jude records that "even the archangel Michael, when he was disputing with the devil about the body of Moses, did not dare to bring a slanderous accusation against him, but said, 'The Lord rebuke you!'" (Jude 1:9). Think about it! Not even an archangel like Michael would dare to slander Satan. Yet our victory is in Jesus Christ. He has already won. When we confront strongholds of evil, we should rebuke Satan and his demons in the name of Jesus Christ, King of Kings and Lord of Lords.

IV. The Spiritual Warfare

The Lord has called us to spiritual warfare. After Peter made his famous (and first) confession of faith in Jesus as the Messiah in Matthew 16:18, Jesus responded, "And I tell you that you are Peter, and on this rock I will build my church, and the gates of Hades will not overcome it." What kind of weapon is a gate? It is not a weapon but a defensive fortification.

We should be on the offensive. We should assault the kingdom of darkness to rescue those who are in Satan's clutches and bring them to the kingdom of light. Yet, you can bet that when were obedient to the Lord's call, Satan hates it and he fights back. If we have not suffered persecution at all since becoming a believer, we ought to examine ourselves to see if we are truly in the faith. Paul told his disciple Timothy, "In fact, everyone who wants to live a godly life in Christ Jesus will be persecuted, while evil men and impostors will go from bad to worse, deceiving and being deceived" (2 Tim. 3:12-13).

In the Gospel of Luke, chapter 10, Jesus sent seventy-two disciples, two by two, to every place and town He was to visit. "The seventy-two returned with joy and said, 'Lord, even the demons submit to us in your name.' Jesus replied, 'I saw Satan fall like lightning from heaven. I have given you authority to trample on snakes and scorpions and to overcome all the power of the enemy; nothing will harm you. However, do not rejoice that the spirits submit to you, but rejoice that your names are written in heaven'" (Luke 10:18-20). Jesus sent His original disciples and now sends us with authority.

We also need to understand that this spiritual warfare is serious business. It ought not to be undertaken lightly. Spiritual warfare has to be conducted in the Spirit. Consider the account in Acts 19:13-16 of men who did not:

> Some Jews who went around driving out evil spirits tried to invoke the name of the Lord Jesus over those who were demon-possessed. They would say, "In the name of Jesus, whom Paul preaches, I command you to come out." Seven sons of Sceva, a Jewish chief priest, were doing this. One day the evil spirit answered them, "Jesus I know, and I know about Paul, but who are you?" Then the man who had the evil spirit jumped on them and overpowered them

all. He gave them such a beating that they ran out of the house naked and bleeding.

These seven sons of Sceva may not have been believers when they attempted this warfare. Regardless, they suffered because they had a flippant view of spiritual warfare.

Clearly, a Christian is called to be a warrior. Yet, we do not fight as the world fights. "For our struggle is not against flesh and blood, but against the rulers, against the authorities, against the powers of this dark world and against the spiritual forces of evil in the heavenly realms" (Eph. 6:12).

The Bible tells us how we are to wage spiritual warfare. We see this in the verses after the one I just quoted from Ephesians 6:

> Therefore put on the full armor of God, so that when the day of evil comes, you may be able to stand your ground, and after you have done everything, to stand. Stand firm then, with the belt of truth buckled around your waist, with the breastplate of righteousness in place, and with your feet fitted with the readiness that comes from the gospel of peace. In addition to all this, take up the shield of faith, with which you can extinguish all the flaming arrows of the evil one. Take the helmet of salvation and the sword of the Spirit, which is the Word of God. And pray in the Spirit on all occasions with all kinds of prayers and requests. With this in mind, be alert and always keep on praying for all the saints.
>
> Ephesians 6:13-18

V. The Serpent's Covenant

Satan does not want us to fight. He will do anything he can to prevent us from being effective for the kingdom of God.

He will try to scare us. He will seduce us into sin, making us ineffective. He will try to lull us into complacency.

This tactic is especially true in the western world where the name-it-and-claim-it, happy-clappy, prosperity gospel is often preached. Many apostate preachers tell their flocks that if they are suffering persecution and are not reaping abundant material blessings, it is because they are outside of God's will. This statement is a false gospel that will lead people to hell. In fact, the Bible says that if we want to lead godly lives in Christ Jesus, we will suffer persecution (2 Tim. 3:12).

Now, let's consider our primary text in 1 Samuel 11. The setting is ancient Israel after the period of the judges. Saul has been anointed king. The town of Jabesh Gilead, which is on the western side of the Jordan, was besieged by Nahash the Ammonite. The Ammonites were descended from Ammon, one of Lot's sons born through incest. Here is the text from 1 Samuel 11:1-13 (NKJV):

> Then Nahash the Ammonite came up and encamped against Jabesh Gilead; and all the men of Jabesh said to Nahash, "Make a covenant with us, and we will serve you."

> And Nahash the Ammonite answered them, "On this condition I will make a covenant with you, that I may put out all your right eyes, and bring reproach on all Israel." Then the elders of Jabesh said to him, "Hold off for seven days, that we may send messengers to all the territory of Israel. And then, if there is no one to save us, we will come out to you."

> So the messengers came to Gibeah of Saul and told the news in the hearing of the people. And all the people lifted up their voices and wept. Now there was Saul, coming behind the herd from the field;

and Saul said, "What troubles the people, that they weep?" And they told him the words of the men of Jabesh.

Then the Spirit of God came upon Saul when he heard this news, and his anger was greatly aroused. So he took a yoke of oxen and cut them in pieces, and sent them throughout all the territory of Israel by the hands of messengers, saying, "Whoever does not go out with Saul and Samuel to battle, so it shall be done to his oxen." And the fear of the Lord fell on the people, and they came out with one consent. When he numbered them in Bezek, the children of Israel were three hundred thousand, and the men of Judah thirty thousand.

And they said to the messengers who came, "Thus you shall say to the men of Jabesh Gilead: 'Tomorrow, by the time the sun is hot, you shall have help.'" Then the messengers came and reported it to the men of Jabesh, and they were glad. Therefore the men of Jabesh said, "Tomorrow we will come out to you, and you may do with us whatever seems good to you."

So it was, on the next day, that Saul put the people in three companies; and they came into the midst of the camp in the morning watch, and killed Ammonites until the heat of the day. And it happened that those who survived were scattered, so that no two of them were left together.

Then the people said to Samuel, "Who is he who said, 'Shall Saul reign over us?' Bring the men, that we may put them to death." But Saul said, "Not a man shall be put to death this day, for today the Lord has accomplished salvation in Israel."

Consider carefully what happened here. Jabesh Gilead was on the western side of the Jordan. It comprised people who were content to stay where they were instead of crossing over the river with the majority of the tribes of Israel into the Promised Land. This may symbolize the one who is reluctant to come completely within God's will.

If there was a town in all of Israel that did not deserve to be rescued, it was Jabesh Gilead. The town had done horribly evil things in the past, and the people did what was right in their own sight. The townspeople had previously horrifically violated a Levite's concubine, and the town was punished severely.

The town, when in grave danger, sent messengers not to Saul, who had already been anointed king and who was awaiting an assignment, but to all Israel. They relied on human strength. They did not acknowledge God's anointing of Saul. It was a rebellious town.[37]

The name Nahash is an Aramaic word, and it means "serpent." Think about what Nahash required in his covenant. All of the men of Jabesh Gilead had to consent to have their right eyes gouged out. That, in itself, would be a great humiliation, but there was a reason for that term of his covenant. A soldier carried his shield in his left hand. He carried his spear in his right hand. His right eye was his fighting eye. He needed it to throw a spear accurately. So Nahash, the serpent, was seeking to render the men unable ever to fight him in the future.

This is exactly what Satan wants to do with us. He wants us to lay down our swords (the Word of God), and never interfere with his possession of other souls destined for hell. If we consent to that, he says he will leave us alone. Satan makes the offer repeatedly. Remember that he is the consummate liar, a fraud and a betrayer.

The townspeople in Jabesh Gilead said that if no one came to rescue them, they would surrender to Nahash. This is symbolic of the one who doubts the salvation of the Lord. "He who doubts is like a wave of the sea, blown and tossed by the wind" (James 1:6).

Yet, Jabesh Gilead was rescued by the mighty working of the Spirit of the Lord through His people. Even after this victory, though, some wanted to kill those who had previously rejected Saul's anointing. Saul, showing the graciousness of the Lord, said that no one would be put to death that day. The Lord pursues us and loves us in spite of our rebelliousness. Satan, however, wants us to lay down our arms, to make a covenant with him, to forsake the spiritual warfare, and to remain securely in his prison. When we are besieged by Satan, all we have to do is cry out "Lord, save me!"

There are numerous other examples of godly men being called to compromise in order to save their own lives. The prophet Daniel was persecuted because he did not honor a decree that prohibited him from praying to the Lord God. He was thrown into the lion's den as a result, but the Lord rescued him.

Likewise, Shadrach, Meshach, and Abednego were thrown into a fiery furnace because they would not bow down to an idol that King Nebuchadnezzar built. They would have been spared the ordeal if they had only fallen down and worshipped the image the king made. Look at the bravery of their response:

> O Nebuchadnezzar, we do not need to defend ourselves before you in this matter. If we are thrown into the blazing furnace, the God we serve is able to save us from it, and he will rescue us from your hand, O king. But even if he does not, we want you

to know, O king, that we will not serve your gods or
worship the image of gold you have set up.

Daniel 3:16-18

They would not waiver in their commitment to the Lord,
even if the Lord chose to let them die.

Men, let us never make peace with the devil. Let us never
agree to his covenant. Let us pursue the battles of the Lord
with vigor. And may you all "put on the full armor of God,
so that when the day of evil comes, you may be able to stand
your ground, and after you have done everything, to stand"
(Eph. 6:13). May God bless you abundantly through the read
of His Word, and may God bring revival to the Estelle Unit.

CHAPTER 9

The Enemy Within

presented by Judge Rick Davis November 19, 2006
during Chapel Service at the Hamilton Unit, Bryan, Texas.

I. Introduction

Men, I consider it a privilege to be here with you this morning and to share with you the good news of Jesus Christ. Some of you may have been here when I came last August to speak to you about the unclaimed pardon that is free for the taking. As I said then and as I say again now, I am no different in the sight of God than any of you are.

In my daily life I work as a judge. Yet, as I stand here before you today, I do not speak to you as a judge, but as one spiritual beggar telling another where to find bread. I am here today to talk to you about the Bread of Life, Jesus Christ.

You see, God's standards of truth and justice are infinitely higher than those of any earthly judge. Not only can God see the bad things that I do, but God sees my thought life. And in God's sight, thinking about adultery is the same as committing it, thinking about murder is the same as doing it, and thinking about stealing is the same in God's sight as actually stealing. No matter what you have done, no matter what crime you may have committed, in God's sight I am just like you: a sinner that desperately needed a Savior.

Therefore, this morning "behold the Lamb of God, which taketh away the sin of the world" (John 1:29 KJV). I preach Jesus Christ crucified, a stumbling block to many and foolishness to many others. Yet "the foolishness of God is wiser than men; and the weakness of God is stronger than men" (1 Cor. 1:25 KJV).

I know that the Hamilton Unit is a pre-release unit. That is to say that I know that all of you expect to be released at some point or another during the next several months. Let me ask for a show of hands, how many of you, once you are released, never want to come back to prison?

We have all heard of recidivism, which means relapse into crime. I recently read reports that say that Texas' recidivism rate is around thirty percent. Some reports say that it is higher, some lower. But for you, men, if you are released and come back into prison, your recidivism rate is one hundred percent.

Today, I want to talk to you about why it is that we still tend to sin or to do wrong, even after we trust Jesus Christ. Today, we will talk about "The Enemy Within." It is my fervent desire to provide you with something useful today, something that may help you after you are released and that will help you live a new life. If you have been locked up for five or ten or more years, you will find that it is a whole new world out there when you get out. The temptations are greater, and it is hard to avoid many of them, no matter how diligent we are.

I know that many of you already believe in Jesus Christ, but some of you may not. It will make little sense to you to talk about overcoming the temptation to sin and walking in the Spirit if you have never been born again in the first place. We will talk about that first.

Men, it is important that we come to grips with the fact that we will all stand before God to give an account for ourselves.

II. The Coming Judgment

In Psalm 9:7, it is written, "The LORD reigns forever; he has established his throne for judgment." Consider also what God says about his own Word: "'Is not my word like fire,' declares the LORD, 'and like a hammer that breaks a rock in pieces?'" (Jer. 23:29).

The Bible says that man is destined to die once, and after that to face judgment (Heb. 9:27). Let's look briefly at what that judgment will be like. Ecclesiastes 12:13-14 reads, "God will bring every deed into judgment, including every hidden thing, whether it is good or evil." Likewise, Isaiah writes:

> See, the LORD is coming with fire, and his chariots are like a whirlwind; he will bring down his anger with fury, and his rebuke with flames of fire.
>
> For with fire and with his sword the LORD will execute judgment upon all men, and many will be those slain by the LORD.
>
> Isaiah 66:15-16

The book of Revelation speaks of who will be thrown into the lake of fire:

> But the cowardly, unbelieving, abominable, murderers, sexually immoral, sorcerers, idolaters, and all liars shall have their part in the lake which burns with fire and brimstone, which is the second death.
>
> Revelation 21:8 NKJV

Finally, in Jeremiah 25:31, it is written:

> "The tumult will resound to the ends of the earth, for the LORD will bring charges against the nations;

he will bring judgment on all mankind and put the wicked to the sword," declares the LORD.

Thus, if you think about it, the judgment of God that is coming upon the earth is terrifying, and we cannot imagine how bad it will be for those who go to eternal punishment. The Bible tells us that those people whose name is not written in the Book of Life will be thrown into the lake of fire (Rev. 20:15). This is why the apostle Paul said, "Knowing therefore the terror of the Lord, we persuade men" (2 Cor. 5:11 KJV).

III. Peace With God

If we think about the coming judgment of God, we should stand in awe, amazement, and fear. Doing so will also enable us to see why it is written, "The fear of the LORD is the beginning of wisdom" (Ps. 111:10).

We should also wonder how we can make peace with such a fearsome, terrifying God. So how do we have peace with God? Many people wrongly think that if one obeys all of God's commandments, God will approve him. The law of God is holy, just, and good, but the handing down of God's law was not primarily intended to give us a moral code by which to live.

In Psalm 19:7 (KJV), it is written, "The law of the Lord is perfect, converting the soul." You see, "By the law comes the knowledge of sin" (Rom 3:20 KJV), and, as the apostle Paul wrote in Romans 7:7: "Indeed I would not have known what sin was except through the law. For I would not have known what coveting really was if the law had not said, 'Do not covet.'"

When Jesus walked the earth, there was a group of religious people in Jerusalem called Pharisees. They were very legalistic, and many of them were really bad hypocrites.

They took pride in the way that they supposedly kept (in their own minds) God's commandments.

The people that Jesus rebuked the most harshly were the religious hypocrites: men who professed to follow God, but who had no true humility or tenderness of heart. Hear what the Lord said in the Gospel of Matthew 23:23 (NKJV):

> Woe to you, scribes and Pharisees, hypocrites! For you pay tithe of mint and anise and cummin, and have neglected the weightier matters of the law: justice and mercy and faith. These you ought to have done, without leaving the others undone.

This verse tells us many things, but let us look at the weightier matters of the law: justice, mercy and faith. You see, God is so holy, so perfect, so just that He must punish sin wherever it is found. His justice will also be absolutely thorough. The Bible says His eyes are too pure to look upon evil. Thus, the law of God demands justice. This is the first of the three weightier matters of the law.

It is written, "For whoever keeps the whole law and yet stumbles at just one point is guilty of breaking all of it" (James 2:10). If we stumble at just one tiny point of violating God's law, we are just as bad as the worst lawbreaker. Thus, the law of God does not help us, it leaves us helpless. We cannot earn good favor in God's sight by even trying our best to obey God's law. It is for this reason that a multitude of people are practically held in slavery because of their fear of death and the coming judgment.

God's law and His justice make us aware that we desperately need God's mercy. This is the second of the three weightier matters of the law. As the apostle Paul wrote to Titus, "When the kindness and love of God our Savior appeared, he saved us, not because of righteous things we had done, but because of his mercy" (Titus 3:4). You see, while God is holy and just, God is also perfect love. God longs to have mercy on us because of His love. He loves us in spite of our sinfulness, but His holiness must be satisfied.

This brings us to third of the three weightier matters of the law: faith. Faith, which is in itself a gift of God, is the means by which we obtain God's mercy. By faith in Jesus Christ, we obtain God's mercy, and we have peace with God. As it is written:

> Therefore, since we have been justified through faith, we have peace with God through our Lord Jesus Christ, through whom we have gained access by faith into this grace in which we now stand. And we rejoice in the hope of the glory of God.
>
> Romans 5:1-2

Therefore, men, "I tell you, now is the time of God's favor, now is the day of salvation" (2 Cor. 6:2). "Today, if you hear his voice, do not harden your hearts" (Heb. 3:15). "If you confess with your mouth, 'Jesus is Lord,' and believe in your heart that God raised him from the dead, you will be saved" (Rom. 10:9).

IV. The False Gospel, Its Resulting Discouragement, and Those Who Depart from the Faith

Men, there are many people today who do not present the gospel in such stark terms as we are considering it in this morning. There are many people that preach what I call "the happy, clappy, name-it-and-claim-it, prosperity gospel." They say, "Give your heart to Jesus; He'll give you love, joy, peace, and happiness. He will help you with your marital problems, your drinking problems, your drug problems," and so forth.

They preach a repentance-free gospel and portray Jesus Christ as the cosmic teddy bear who just wants to give you a big hug. Oftentimes, they also preach automatic prosperity if you believe. They say that if you are a believer and are having any kind of difficulty, financial, marital, health, or otherwise, it must be because you are sinning, or because you do not have enough faith. Such false gospel preachers insult the great many believers throughout the ages who have suffered great persecution and even laid down their lives in blood because of their faith in Jesus Christ. People suffer and die for the gospel even today in many parts of the world.

It is true that Jesus wants our whole hearts; He wants every bit of us. But we have to come to Him in true humility. Jesus Christ is Lord and God. When we approach Him, we deal with the same One who gave us life, who gave us breath, and who gave us everything that we cherish in life. His wisdom, knowledge, and power are so great that He knows how many hairs are on your head and how many billions of stars there are in the universe. He is truly awesome.

Some people actually come to faith in Jesus through this weaker way, through the message that does not address how hideous and horrific our sin is in God's sight, but that is not the way Jesus reached people when He walked the earth. If you consider carefully what He did in the Gospels, you will see that to the proud of heart, Jesus gave the law. To the humble, He showed grace. With the law, God breaks the hard heart. With the gospel, God heals the broken heart. As it is written, "The sacrifices of God are a broken spirit; a broken and contrite heart, O God, you will not despise" (Ps. 51:17).

There is a reason that I talk about the gospel before getting to the main point of the talk: the enemy within. The preaching of a false gospel or less than the whole gospel leads to false conversions. The Bible tells us that in latter times, some will depart from the faith (1 Tim. 4:11). The false teachers cannot tell you why that is, and they cannot tell you how to ensure that you are not such a person.

The Bible is also very clear that many people will die expecting heaven but receiving hell. Frankly, I think that the most dreadful words that the human ear could ever hear would be to stand before God after death and to hear Jesus say, "Get away from me, I never knew you." The most blessed and wonderful words that we can hear are for Jesus to say to us after we die, "Well done, good and faithful servant ...Come and share your master's happiness" (Matt. 25:21).

When the disciples questioned Jesus about the parable of the sower and the four soils, He said "Don't you understand this parable? How then will you understand any parable?" (Mark 4:13). You see, the parable of the four soils and the sower is a key parable that unlocks the mystery to several other parables.

In this parable we see the unbeliever, the false convert, the believer who has become unfruitful for God, and the believer who is living for God in every way. The seed sown on rocky soil represents the one who turns away from God. Jesus said of him:

> Others, like seed sown on rocky places, hear the word and at once receive it with joy. But since they have no root, they last only a short time. When trouble or persecution comes because of the word, they quickly fall away.
>
> Mark 4:16-17

The false gospel preachers, because they have not preached the whole counsel of God, mislead people into professing faith in Jesus so that they only view Him as a cosmic genie in a bottle who promises a life of ease and happiness. Such people come to Jesus Christ for wish fulfillment and freedom from hardship, but to the contrary, the

Bible says, "Everyone who wants to live a godly life in Christ Jesus will be persecuted" (2 Tim. 3:12).

When we believe in Jesus Christ, we are not promised a life of ease. We are promised four things: temptation, tribulation, persecution, and eternal life. Our lives on this earth may still be really hard, but He promises to be there with us through it all. God has said in His word, "Never will I leave you; never will I forsake you" (Heb. 13:5). When the Israelites left Egypt in the desert, they came upon a place called Marah which had water, but the water was bitter. When they grumbled to Moses, the Lord showed Moses a piece of wood. He threw it into the bitter water, and the bitter water became sweet.

When we believe in Jesus Christ, we have eternal life. Our earthly lives do not necessarily become easy, but we have the wood that the Lord shows us that makes our bitter waters sweet. That wood is the cross of Jesus Christ.

V. The Threefold Nature of Man

Men, thus far we have talked about the coming judgment of God and how to obtain peace with God through faith in Jesus Christ. We have talked about the false gospel and false converts. Yet we still have not talked about conquering the enemy within. Well, we need to cover one more area before we get there, and that area deals with the makeup of man.

Man is composed of essentially three parts: body (which includes the flesh), soul, and spirit. When Paul blessed the Thessalonians at the end of his first letter to them (1 Thessalonians 5:23), he wrote:

May God himself, the God of peace, sanctify you through and through. May your whole *spirit, soul and body* be kept blameless at the coming of our Lord Jesus Christ (emphasis added).

We see a contrast between soul and spirit also in Hebrews 4:12-13, which reads:

> For the Word of God is living and active. Sharper than any double-edged sword, it penetrates even to dividing *soul and spirit*, joints and marrow; it judges the thoughts and attitudes of the heart (emphasis added).

The Greek word that is translated as "spirit" in the verses is *pneuma. Pneuma* also means wind. From it we get the English words pneumonia, an illness that affects the lungs, and pneumatic, moved by air. Some of you may have experience as auto mechanics and have operated pneumatically driven tools. They are air-powered.

The Greek word that is translated as "soul" is *psyche.* From it we get the English words psychiatry, psychology, psychic, psychopath, and the like.

Many verses throughout the New Testament talk about the flesh. The Greek word that is translated as "flesh" is *sarx.* From it we get the English word sarcasm, a bitter form of ridicule that literally means "to bite the lips in rage." We also get the word sarcophagus, a word for a tomb that literally means "flesh eating."

The body is composed of flesh. The word that is translated "body" is *soma*, and from it we get the word psychosomatic, which refers to physical, bodily symptoms that are caused by the mind. Note that in the New International Version, the Greek word *sarx* is often translated as "sinful nature," which is more an explanation than it is a translation. Thus, we are tripartite (or three part) beings comprising spirit, soul, and flesh (which is within the body).

The soul, one of the three parts, itself comprises the mind, will, and emotions. Before we are saved, our soul is subject to Satan, the spirit of disobedience (see Eph. 2:1-2), and our soul is also subject to the passions of the flesh. It is through our flesh that we relate to the world. We perceive the world through our five senses, and our flesh operates on our souls. It is written of man's creation:

> And the LORD God formed man of the dust of the ground, and breathed into his nostrils the breath of life; and man became a living soul.
>
> Genesis 2:7 KJV

When man was originally created, the soul was like the intersection of the spirit of God and the material world taken up in the flesh. When Adam sinned, he died. Although he did not physically die until many years later, his spirit died within him at the time of man's fall.

Thus, our souls are subject to the bondage of the spirit of disobedience from within and the passions of the flesh from without: the double whammy. This subjection is why we are absolutely without hope unless God himself calls us to Him. Jesus said, "No one can come to me unless the Father who sent me draws him, and I will raise him up at the last day" (John 6:44). We are literally and truly spiritually blind, and we cannot possibly see or understand the things of God unless He reveals them to us and draws us to Him first.

In fact, until God did a work in our hearts, Jesus Christ and His death, burial, and resurrection seemed foolishness to us. As the apostle Paul said:

> But the natural man does not receive the things of the Spirit of God, for they are foolishness to him; nor can he know them, because they are spiritually discerned.
>
> 1 Corinthians 2:14 KJV

In this verse from the King James Version, the Greek word translated "natural" is *psychikos*, and the Greek word translated "spiritually" is *pneumatikos*. Another valid way to translate this verse would be to say:

> But the "soulish" man [or the man thinking and operating only out of his soul] does not receive the things of the Spirit of God, for they are foolishness to him; nor can he know them, because they are spiritually discerned.

It is through God's enabling that we can understand these things, and we see why Jesus said, "No one can see the kingdom of God unless he is born again" (John 3:3). Paul wrote to the Christians in Galatia and mourned for them because they were falling back into useless, godless legalism. He said, "I am again in the pains of childbirth until Christ is *formed* in you" (Gal. 4:19, emphasis added).

If we believe, we are being conformed to the image of the Son of God, and He is being formed within us. Upon conversion, the Spirit of God enters our souls similar to the way a sperm cell enters an egg cell and creates new life. There is much spiritual symbolism in human sexuality, but we will have to save that for some other time. For now, we can see that the Spirit of Jesus Christ has to enter our souls for us to be saved. This is the meaning of being born again.

In Peter's first epistle, he wrote, "For you are receiving the goal of your faith, the salvation of your souls" (1 Pet. 1:9). Yet all of us will physically die sooner or later. Our corrupted flesh has to die. But if we are saved, our souls will have eternal life, and at the resurrection, we will be given glorified bodies.

VI. The Enemy Within

With this foundation established, we can now talk about the enemy within, and the problem of indwelling sin within the believer.

When you get out into the free world, you will find temptations galore. Satan will tempt you the worst with what God hates most. Do you remember the verse we discussed earlier about those who would have their part in the lake of fire? The Greek word that is translated "sorcerers" in Revelation 21:8 is *pharmakeus*, from which we get the English word pharmacy. There can be no doubt here that the Bible refers to illegal drug use and illegal drug dealers. The Greek word that is translated "sexually immoral" is *pornos*, from which we get the English word pornography. One of Satan's most potent tools to bring a man down is illicit sexuality.

Now, don't think that being a Christian is a life of "shall nots." In Psalm 16:11, it is written, "You have made known to me the path of life; you will fill me with joy in your presence, with *eternal pleasures* at your right hand" (emphasis added). God wants to bless us and to overwhelm us with pleasure. Remember that God intentionally put man into the Garden of Eden. The Hebrew word "Eden" means "pleasure."

Remember also that God invented sex. He created it to teach us about the holy relationship between Jesus Christ and His bride, the church. He also created it for the enjoyment of men and women in a marriage relationship.

If man is the crown of God's creation, then woman is the jewel that adorns the crown. In fact, there is nothing more beautiful in all of God's creation than woman. God gave human beings sexuality for a husband and wife to enjoy completely. Read the book in the Bible called Song of Solomon. It is a passionate book about the love between a husband and wife. The only time that God speaks to the lovers in the entire book is to command them to drink deeply of their love for each other: "Drink, yes, drink deeply, O beloved ones!" (Song of Sol. 5:1 NKJV).

He also gave human beings sexuality to teach us about the relationship of the church to Jesus Christ. We will talk more about the deep symbolism of marriage later, but remember that Satan is an expert at taking the good things that God gave mankind and perverting them in rebellion against God.

Just because you believe in Jesus Christ, you should not think that life will be easy for you when you get out. In fact, Satan hates you with a passion and wants to make you stumble. You will be tempted with drugs, pornography, loose women, alcohol, materialism, you name it.

Satan wants to bring you down. Oftentimes, a new believer, excited with his newfound joy in the Lord, wants to "live for Christ," or to strive to be more Christ-like. This desire will last for a while, a few months, maybe even a year, before he realizes that though he wants to live a life pleasing to God, he fails miserably and repeatedly. Consider some of the struggles St. Augustine endured that he recorded in his book *Confessions*:

> In misery my soul cast about, seeking sensual objects that could scratch where the pox itched. Yet there was no love to be found. None of these things had a soul, so they could not be objects of love.

> To love then, and to be loved, was sweet to me. But when I found someone I loved, I wanted only to possess and enjoy the body of the person I loved. I found a spring of friendship and polluted it with lascivious filth. I veiled the brightness of real love with a hell of foul, unseemly lust.[38]

Consider also the struggles that Martin Luther endured that he described in a letter to his good friend, Melanchthon, while cooped up in the castle at Wartburg (it was during this period that Luther translated the New Testament into German so that the common people could understand it):

> I sit here at ease, hardened and unfeeling– alas! Praying little, grieving little for the Church of God, burning rather in the fierce fires of my untamed flesh. It comes to this: I should be afire in the spirit; in reality I am afire in the flesh, with lust, laziness, idleness, sleepiness....[39]

Even a great lover of Jesus Christ like the apostle Paul found that he could not do any good on his own. Spend some time dwelling on Romans 7:14-25 (NKJV). Hear what Paul says in that passage:

> For we know that the law is spiritual, but I am carnal, sold under sin. For what I am doing, I do not understand. For what I will to do, that I do not practice; but what I hate, that I do. If, then, I do what I will not to do, I agree with the law that it is good. But now, it is no longer I who do it, but sin that dwells in me. For I know that in me (that is, in my flesh) nothing good dwells; for to will is present with me, but how to perform what is good I do not find. For the good that I will to do, I do not do; but the evil I will not to do, that I practice. Now if I do what I will not to do, it is no longer I who do it, but sin that dwells in me.
>
> I find then a law, that evil is present with me, the one who wills to do good. For I delight in the law of God according to the inward man. But I see another law in my members, warring against the law of my mind, and bringing me into captivity to the law of sin which is in my members. O wretched man that I am!

Who will deliver me from this body of death? I thank God—through Jesus Christ our Lord! So then, with the mind I myself serve the law of God, but with the flesh the law of sin.

Paul recognized that the flesh lusts against the Spirit, and the Spirit lusts against the flesh (Gal. 5:15 KJV). Thus, our souls are the battleground between God and Satan. Consider what the Lord Jesus says about our souls. In John 12:25, it is written: "He who loves his life will lose it, and he who hates his life in this world will keep it for eternal life."

Men, the Greek word here translated "life" in the first two instances in this verse is *psyche*, and this is the way these two words in this verse are translated in every modern English translation of the Bible. I think that this is unfortunate, and we lose something in the English translation. The Greek word most often translated "life" in the New Testament is *zoe*, and it occurs in the New Testament 134 times. *Zoe* is the word that is translated "life" in the third instance in this particular verse. The word *psyche* is translated as "soul" more times than it is translated as "life."

What did Jesus mean when He said what He did in John 12:25? He did not mean that we should hate our life in such a way that we want to commit suicide: far from it. He said that we have to hate our soul in this world so that we may keep it for eternal life (*zoe*).

Why should we hate our souls in this world? It is because we know that even though we are beginning to understand how great the salvation of God is and how much He loves us, we still have this tendency to fall back into the sins of the flesh. Our souls have a tendency to turn back to the flesh and away from the Spirit of God within us. For that we truly should mourn. I think that this is what Paul meant when he wrote the Corinthians that he was "sorrowful, yet always rejoicing" (1 Cor. 6:10).

If you have not ever read the Bible in its entirety, I urge you to do so soon. I guarantee you that you will be blessed if you read it with an open mind, an honest heart, and an earnest prayer before God that He teach you through it. In the meantime, until you have read the whole thing, I would recommend that you read first the Gospel of John. There you will clearly see the passion of Jesus Christ for you.

Then, read the book of Genesis. That book is foundational to so many other books in the Bible.

After that, read the book of Romans. Read it two or three times. Meditate upon it. Chew on it. Think about it. The book of Romans contains a most comprehensive overview of Christianity and what salvation through faith means. There, you will understand that we do not have and can never have any righteousness that is pleasing to God in and of ourselves and apart from the grace of Jesus Christ.

In the first five chapters of Romans, Paul tells us how God delivers us from our sins. In chapters six and seven, he tells us how we are delivered from our sinful nature, that is, our continual tendency to sin. In chapter eight, he tells us about being led by the Spirit of God (Rom. 8:1-17 NKJV):

> There is therefore now no condemnation to those who are in Christ Jesus, who do not walk according to the flesh, but according to the Spirit. For the law of the Spirit of life in Christ Jesus has made me free from the law of sin and death. For what the law could not do in that it was weak through the flesh, God did by sending His own Son in the likeness of sinful flesh, on account of sin: He condemned sin in the flesh, that the righteous requirement of the law might be fulfilled in us who do not walk according to the flesh but according to the Spirit.

For those who live according to the flesh set their minds on the things of the flesh, but those who live according to the Spirit, the things of the Spirit. For to be carnally minded is death, but to be spiritually minded is life and peace. Because the carnal mind is enmity against God; for it is not subject to the law of God, nor indeed can be. So then, those who are in the flesh cannot please God.

But you are not in the flesh but in the Spirit, if indeed the Spirit of God dwells in you. Now if anyone does not have the Spirit of Christ, he is not His. And if Christ is in you, the body is dead because of sin, but the Spirit is life because of righteousness. But if the Spirit of Him who raised Jesus from the dead dwells in you, He who raised Christ from the dead will also give life to your mortal bodies through His Spirit who dwells in you.

Therefore, brethren, we are debtors—not to the flesh, to live according to the flesh. For if you live according to the flesh you will die; but if by the Spirit you put to death the deeds of the body, you will live. For as many as are led by the Spirit of God, these are sons of God. For you did not receive the spirit of bondage again to fear, but you received the Spirit of adoption by whom we cry out, "Abba, Father." The Spirit Himself bears witness with our spirit that we are children of God, and if children, then heirs—heirs of God and joint heirs with Christ, if indeed we suffer with Him, that we may also be glorified together.

The way to keep sin consistently out of your life (and the temptation to commit new crimes) is by continually looking to Jesus in humility, brokenness, and joy. If you keep your eyes on Him, He will choke out the sin. But you have to yield to Him in humility. "For if you live according to the flesh you will die; but if by the Spirit you put to death the deeds of the body, you will live" (Rom. 8:13).

Men, we have to die to ourselves. We have to recognize that within ourselves, there is no good thing. Apart from the work of God within us, we are worthless. Consider this way of looking at it in a quote from Andrew Murray's book *Humility*:

> If you would enter into full fellowship with Christ in His death, and know the full deliverance from self, humble yourself. This is your one duty. Place yourself before God in your utter helplessness; consent heartily to the fact of your impotence to slay or make alive yourself; sink down into your own nothingness, in the spirit of meek and patient and trustful surrender to God. Accept every humiliation. Look upon every fellow-man who tries or vexes you, as a means of grace to humble you. Use every opportunity of humbling yourself before your fellow-men as a help to abide humble before God. God will accept such humbling of yourself as the proof that your whole heart desires it, as the very best prayer for it, as your preparation for His mighty work of grace, when, by the mighty strengthening of His Holy Spirit, He reveals Christ fully in you, so that He, in His form of a servant, is truly formed in you, and dwells in your heart. It is the path of humility which leads to perfect death, the full and perfect experience that we are dead in Christ.[40]

The way to walk with God and to turn your back on temptation is not to strive to be good. If that is the approach you take, you will fail eventually every time. The way to do it is to surrender continually to God in humility and to admit that you can do no good. When temptation arises, pray in your mind to God, "Lord, this temptation is too powerful for me. I cannot resist it. Yet, I want to resist it. Lord, I am asking you to resist it for me and through me."

Let me give you two examples that may help you. If you have an empty bottle, do you know the best way to get all of the air out of it? You may think to put a high-powered vacuum on it that has a leak-proof seal. That requires a lot of work, and a leak will form sooner or later anyway. The best way to get all the air out of a bottle is to fill the bottle with something else, a liquid like water. It takes no effort.

Here is another example. How many of you have ever had a lawn with St. Augustine grass in it? Ever had a lawn with St. Augustine that also had a lot of big ugly clumps of Johnson grass in it? What is the best way to get rid of the weeds? You can spend hours every day pulling the weeds, and they will always come back. The best way to get rid of the weeds is to fertilize the good grass, and the good grass will choke out the weeds. Just try it when you get out, and you will see what I mean.

We have to surrender to God, and trust the Lord completely. We need to die to self in order to experience a deeper life in Christ, what the great preacher, Andrew Murray, called "the Second Blessing." I cannot say it better than he did in his book entitled *Covenants and Blessings* (from Note A):

Conversion makes of a sinner a child of God, full of ignorance and weakness, without any conception of what the whole-hearted devotion is that God asks of him, or the full possession God is ready to take of him. In some cases the transition from the elementary stage is by a gradual growth and enlightenment. But experience teaches, that in the great majority of cases this healthy growth is not found. To those who have never found the secret of a healthy growth, of victory over sin and perfect rest in God, and have possibly despaired of ever finding it, because all their efforts have been failures, it has often been a wonderful help to learn that it is possible by a single decisive step, bringing them into a right relationship to Christ, His Spirit, and His strength, to enter upon an entirely new life.

What is needed to help a man to take that step is very simple. He must see and confess the wrongness, the sin, of the life he is living, not in harmony with God's will. He must see and believe in the life which Scripture holds out, which Christ Jesus promises to work and maintain in him. As he sees that his failure has been owing to his striving in his own strength, and believes that our Lord Jesus will actually work all in him in Divine power, he takes courage, and dares surrender himself to Christ anew. Confessing and giving up all that is of self and sin, yielding himself wholly to Christ and His service, he believes and receives a new power to live his life by the faith of the Son of God. The change is in many cases as clear, as marked, as wonderful, as conversion. For lack of a better name, that of A Second Blessing came most naturally.[41]

VII. The Desire of God

Men, as you grow closer and closer to God through Jesus Christ and as you study His Word, you will realize that the Bible is God's love letter to you. Jesus laid down His life for those who believe to make the perfect sacrifice that would satisfy God's holy justice and let us have peace with God. When Jesus Christ died on the cross, a Roman stuck a spear in His side. Out of the wound flowed blood, which signifies the redemption for sin, and water, which signifies the life giving Spirit.

In the second chapter of the Bible, we read about the first husband and the first wife. When God created Eve, the suitable bride for Adam, He put Adam into a deep sleep and opened his side to create a wife for him. Eve was Adam's wife. Eve was made of the same stuff as Adam. In the same way, God put Jesus Christ into the deep sleep of death and opened His side to create a bride for Him. That bride is the church. The church is the wife of Christ. We are remade with the same Spirit of Jesus Christ. In the second to last chapter of the last book in the Bible, it is written:

> Then I saw a new heaven and a new earth, for the first heaven and the first earth had passed away, and there was no longer any sea. I saw the Holy City, the New Jerusalem, coming down out of heaven from God, prepared as a bride beautifully dressed for her husband. And I heard a loud voice from the throne saying, "Now the dwelling of God is with men, and he will live with them. They will be his people, and God himself will be with them and be their God. He will wipe every tear from their eyes. There will be no more death or mourning or crying or pain, for the old order of things has passed away."
>
> Revelation 21:1-4

Men, if you are believers in Jesus Christ, you are part of the bride of Christ. Let us endeavor to draw closer and closer to God evermore. We cannot please God by trying to do good. We cannot do good at all, even after we are believers. The Bible says, "Everything that does not come from faith is sin" (Rom. 14:23b).

Therefore, let us sink deeper and deeper into the death of Christ, putting to death the deeds of the flesh by submitting to the Spirit of God. Let us walk by faith, not by sight. As Paul said to the Galatian church, "I have been crucified with Christ and I no longer live, but Christ lives in me. The life I live in the body, I live by faith in the Son of God, who loved me and gave himself for me" (Gal. 2:20).

May God bless the reading and study of His Word this morning. And men, may God bless you now and in days to come. May He draw you ever closer into a deeper relationship with Himself.

CHAPTER 10

Signs of the Times and the Day of the Lord

Presented by Rick Davis November 22, 2005
to TAX Chapter at the Estelle Unit, Huntsville, Texas.

—⚏—

I. As One Beggar to Another

Friends, before we begin the primary message, I want to introduce myself. I know many of you, but there are some of you whom I have not had the privilege of meeting. As a judge, I deal with and administer the laws of man every week. But let us consider for a moment God's law.

God gave us His holy law, which makes us painfully and dreadfully aware of our need for a Savior. In Romans 7:13, it is written, "The law is holy, and the commandment is holy, righteous and good." Likewise, in Psalm 19:7, it is written, "The law of the LORD is perfect, reviving the soul. The statutes of the LORD are trustworthy, making wise the simple." The law was not designed to help us; no, the law of God leaves us helpless. As it is written in Romans 3:19-20:

> Now we know that whatever the law says, it says to those who are under the law, so that every mouth may

be silenced and the whole world held accountable to God. Therefore no one will be declared righteous in his sight by observing the law; rather, through the law we become conscious of sin.

Do you see, friends, that with the law of God, God shows us our true selves, that we are wretched, sinful, and evil. In Ezekiel 37:12-14, it is written:

This is what the Sovereign LORD says: O my people, I am going to open your graves and bring you up from them; I will bring you back to the land of Israel. Then you, my people, will know that I am the LORD, when I open your graves and bring you up from them. I will put my Spirit in you and you will live, and I will settle you in your own land. Then you will know that I the LORD have spoken, and I have done it, declares the LORD.

When God wants to show us the wretchedness of sin, He opens our graves. That is, He shows our wretchedness to us within ourselves! Consider the words of Oswald Chambers, that great missionary to the English and Australian troops during World War I. He died while serving in Egypt at age forty-three.

His love for the Lord was deep and he led many souls to Christ. He was well loved by the troops. Fifteen books are attributed to him, most of which were published by his widow after his death. He is best known for his work *My Utmost for His Highest*, the world's most popular devotional. In the devotional for June 1st, Chambers wrote:

When God wants to show you what human nature is like apart from Himself, He has to show it you in yourself. If the Spirit of God has given you a vision of what you are apart from the grace of God (and He only does it when His Spirit is at work), you know there is no criminal who is half so bad in actuality as you know yourself to be in possibility. My "grave" has been opened by God and "I know that in me (that is, in my flesh) dwelleth no good thing." God's Spirit continually reveals what human nature is like apart from His grace.[42]

Chambers was exactly right. Do you see what this means, men? God sees my thought life. No matter what any of you have done to get yourselves here, no matter how bad the crime, I know in my heart of hearts that I am no better than any of you.

I was a vile sinner in desperate need of a Savior. I am a man just like you and no better than you. Thus, when you hear this message, don't think of me as a judge. I am one spiritual beggar telling another where to find bread. By beggar, I mean from one who has been humbled by God and broken by His law.

It is my fervent hope and prayer that this message blesses you. We are living in perilous times, and it important for us to understand the things that are coming upon the earth.

II. Our Nation's Foundations

A great many people came to this country in its early years so that they could have the freedom to worship God with a clear conscience as the Lord led them. In 2 Corinthians 3:17, it is written, "Now the Lord is the Spirit, and where the Spirit of the Lord is, there is freedom." I am convinced that this is why God so abundantly blessed this nation in its first two hundred years, because this nation was founded largely by men and women who fervently sought after God.

Let's consider our roots. The last sentence of the Declaration of Independence reads, "We mutually pledge our lives, our fortunes and our sacred honor." Many of the signers of the declaration gave their lives in the cause or later died as paupers. These were men who gave their all to secure freedom for us.

Consider Patrick Henry. On March 23, 1775, the second Virginia Convention met in Saint John's Church in Richmond, Virginia. The convention moved that the colony be armed. In defense of this move, Patrick Henry said, "Gentlemen may cry Peace! Peace! – but there is no peace! The war is actually begun...Is life so dear, or peace so sweet, as to be purchased at the price of chains and slavery? Forbid it, Almighty God! I know not what course what others may take; but as for me, give me liberty or give me death!"

Consider Captain Isaac Davis and the first revolutionary battle fought at the Old North Bridge near Concord, Massachusetts. It was called the "shot heard round the world."[43] On April 19, 1775, Captain Davis was asked if he was afraid to lead his Acton, Massachusetts minute company and the colonial column "into the middle of the town (Concord) for its defense or die in the attempt". He replied, "No, I am not and I haven't a man that is!"[44]

In a gallant effort reminiscent of King David running to the battle with Goliath, Captain Davis drew his sword, wheeled his company from the line to the right and proceeded down the hill to the causeway leading to the Old North Bridge. During the ensuing fight, Captain Davis was killed immediately, but he roused the courage of the colonial troops. Isaac Davis was the first colonial officer to die in the American Revolution.

The name of the first officer killed fighting for our freedom is very interesting. The name Davis is derived from Davison which is derived from Davidson. Davidson is a contraction of "David's son." This, in turn, is derived from "son of David."

King David was a man after God's own heart, and Jesus Christ's human lineage can be traced back through King David. In the Bible, Isaac was Abraham's son, and he was the son of the promise, that is, God's promise to make Abraham into a great nation. In Genesis we read that God called Abraham to sacrifice Isaac. Abraham was willing to do so, but God stayed his hand at the last minute.

Thus, at the first battle of the American Revolution, a man whose first name was taken from the son of the promise and whose last name signified a man after God's own heart died so that we may be free. Isaac Davis laid down his life for his friends.

These and many other brave men and women laid down their lives in blood so that we could be a free nation. Jesus said, "Greater love has no one than this, that he lay down his life for his friends" (John 15:13). Jesus laid down his life for us so that we could have eternal freedom. In a similar way, many of our founding fathers laid down their lives so that we could have earthly freedom.

Men, let me encourage you in this. Many of you have been here a long, long time. Many of you will stay here for a long time. I know that some of you mourn over this and long for your freedom. Yet, please understand that you have a profound freedom that you may not fully know and appreciate.

In many countries around the world, it is illegal to possess a Bible or to tell anyone about Jesus. In communist China and North Korea, Christians are severely persecuted. They have to meet and worship in secret. For many of them, the only Scriptures that they can have in prison are verses that they have memorized.

I read last week an article in *Voice of the Martyrs* about a Chinese woman who was shot simply for possessing a Bible. Please give thanks to God that, even though you don't have the liberty that you want, you have great liberty to read and study the Word of God. The freedoms for which our fathers fought extend even down to you here in prison.

George Washington said in his first inaugural address, "It would be peculiarly improper to omit in this first official act my fervent supplications to that Almighty Being who rules over the universe, who presides in the councils of nations, and whose providential aids can supply every human defect, that His benediction may consecrate to the liberties and happiness of the people of the United States a Government instituted by themselves for these essential purposes."

George Washington was a God fearing man. As a nation, we have wandered away from our godly heritage in spite of God's abundant blessing.

Consider this proclamation made by another great American and God-fearing man, Abraham Lincoln.

> It is the duty of nations as well as of men to own their dependence upon the overruling power of God: to confess their sins and transgressions in humble sorrow, yet with assured hope that genuine repentance will lead to mercy and pardon; and to recognize the sublime truth, announced in the Holy Scriptures and proven by all history, that those nations are blessed whose God is the Lord.

> We know that by His divine law, nations, like individuals, are subjected to punishments and chastisements in this world. May we not justly fear that the awful calamity of civil war which now desolates the land may be a punishment inflicted upon us for our presumptuous sins, to the needful end of our national reformation as a whole people?

> We have been the recipients of the choicest bounties of heaven; we have been preserved these many

years in peace and prosperity; we have grown in numbers, wealth and power as no other nation has ever grown.

But we have forgotten God. We have forgotten the gracious hand which preserved us in peace and multiplied and enriched and strengthened us, and we have vainly imagined, in the deceitfulness of our hearts, that all these blessings were produced by some superior wisdom and virtue of our own. Intoxicated with unbroken success, we have become too self-sufficient to feel the necessity of redeeming and preserving grace, too proud to pray to the God that made us.

Abraham Lincoln made that statement on October 3, 1863. It was part of the Thanksgiving Day proclamation. He concluded by saying:

It has seemed to me fit and proper that God should be solemnly, reverently, and gratefully acknowledged, as with one heart and one voice, by the whole American people. I do therefore invite my fellow citizens in every part of the United States, and also those who are at sea and those who are sojourning in foreign lands, to set apart and observe the last Thursday of November as a day of Thanksgiving and praise to our beneficent Father who dwelleth in the heavens.

We owe many of our blessings in this nation to the sacrifice of godly men and women who went before us. Although it is popular and fashionable for current leaders to invoke the name of God and to ask for the help of God in our many disasters and calamities, one thing for which Lincoln called that is usually lacking in today's pleas to the nation that invoke the name of God is repentance. God will hold us to account for rebelling against Him.

III. Man's Rebellion Against God's Discipline

The people of this nation and of this world are unwilling to turn from their wicked ways. We, as a people, are stiff necked, and we are just like the stubborn, ungodly people in ancient times when God tried to get their attention.

Think about the people of the earth at the tower of Babel after the great flood of Noah's day. In Genesis 11:1-3, it is written:

> Now the whole world had one language and a common speech. As men moved eastward, they found a plain in Shinar and settled there. They said to each other, "Come, let's make bricks and bake them thoroughly." They used brick instead of stone, and tar for mortar. Then they said, "Come, let us build ourselves a city, with a tower that reaches to the heavens, so that we may make a name for ourselves and not be scattered over the face of the whole earth."

Do you notice anything peculiar here? Have you ever seen a brick house that used tar for mortar? Why would they use tar for mortar between the bricks? Tar is waterproof! They wanted to protect themselves from another flood even though the flood of Noah's day was sent by God!

The ancient Israelites showed the same type of stubbornness. Isaiah 9:8-10 refers to Israel's resistance to God's judgments upon it. There it is written (in the KJV):

> The Lord sent a word into Jacob, and it hath lighted upon Israel. And all the people shall know, even Ephraim and the inhabitants of Samaria, that say, in

the pride and stoutness of heart, the bricks are fallen down, but we will build with hewn stones: the sycamores are cut down, but we will change them into cedars.

This stubbornness and rebelliousness against God's judgments naturally occurs in the hearts of all men. I cannot improve on Matthew Henry's commentary on this passage, so I will quote it here:

They *say, in the pride and stoutness of their heart,* (emphasis mine) Let God himself do his worst; we will hold our own, and make our part good with him. If he ruin our houses, we will repair them, and make them stronger and finer than they were before. Our landlord shall not turn us out of doors, though we pay him no rent, but we will keep in possession. If the houses that were built of bricks be demolished in the war, we will rebuild them with hewn stones, that shall not so easily be thrown down. If the enemy cut down the sycamores, we will plant cedars in the room of them. We will make a hand of God's judgments, gain by them, and so outbrave them. Note, those are ripening apace for ruin whose hearts are unhumbled under humbling providences; for God will walk contrary to those who thus walk contrary to him and provoke him to jealousy, as if they were stronger than he.[45]

Friends, what do we see happening in this country after calamity has been brought upon us? We'll build stronger levees in New Orleans! We will have tighter security at our airports! We will go after the terrorists! How rare it is for us to hear anyone calling for nationwide repentance from our evil deeds as Abraham Lincoln once did!

Yet, God said in 2 Chronicles 7:14, "If my people, who are called by my name, will humble themselves and pray and seek my face and turn from their wicked ways, then will I hear from heaven and will forgive their sin and will heal their land." We should pray God will give us a spirit of repentance. Pray, as the Quakers used to pray, that God will give us the gift of tears.

IV. Prophecies of Future Events

God is very gracious to us in that He always warns us like a loving father, especially when His judgment is coming. Prophecy is a lamp for us to give us light and hope in an ever darkening world. Psalm 119:105 reads, "Your word is a lamp to my feet and a light for my path." Further, it is written in 2 Peter 1:19-21:

> And we have the word of the prophets made more certain, and you will do well to pay attention to it, as to a *light shining in a dark place*, until the day dawns and the morning star rises in your hearts. Above all, you must understand that no prophecy of Scripture came about by the prophet's own interpretation. For prophecy never had its origin in the will of man, but men spoke from God as they were carried along by the Holy Spirit (emphasis added).

Let us also seek God's wisdom in understanding the signs of the times. Many Christians ignore prophecy. Many are intimidated by it. Many Christians hesitate to look at the signs because they don't want to be misled by false prophets (Jesus tells us to watch out for false prophets).

Many hesitate to consider signs in the heavens because they think doing so is the same thing as astrology, which God finds revolting. Astrology (that is, believing that our destinies are controlled by stars) and legitimately discerning the signs are not the same thing. In fact, God intended for us to consider signs. In Genesis 1:14-15, we read:

And God said, "Let there be lights in the expanse of the sky to separate the day from the night, and let them serve as signs to mark seasons and days and years, and let them be lights in the expanse of the sky to give light on the earth." And it was so.

And in Psalm 19:1-3, we read:

The heavens declare the glory of God; the skies proclaim the work of his hands. Day after day they pour forth speech; night after night they display knowledge. There is no speech or language where their voice is not heard.

Some may ask whether we can know when the day of the Lord will come. Some may say that it is not possible to know. Clearly, we cannot know the day or the hour that the Lord will appear again. The Bible is very clear on that in many places. Yet we can know the "season" of the Lord's return. Paul told the Thessalonians, a group of Christians who thought that the Lord had already come, the following in 1 Thessalonians 5:1-5:

Now, brothers, about times and dates we do not need to write to you, for you know very well that the day of the Lord will come like a thief in the night. While people are saying, "Peace and safety," destruction will come on them suddenly, as labor pains on a pregnant woman, and they will not escape. But you, brothers, are not in darkness so that this day should surprise you like a thief. You are all sons of the light and sons of the day. We do not belong to the night or to the darkness.

Matthew 24, Mark 14, and Luke 21 all contain a detailed description of what will come upon the earth in the last days. The Lord would not have told us these things unless He wanted us to pay attention to them. In Mark 13:28-29, it is written:

Now learn this lesson from the fig tree: As soon as its twigs get tender and its leaves come out, you know that summer is near. Even so, when you see these things happening, you know that it is near, right at the door.

Here, Jesus even tells us to learn a lesson from this sign. Now, we have this one great safeguard. If anyone ever says that something is a sign but what he says is contrary to Scripture, then we know it is not true. The Word of the Lord is perfect, flawless, and without error. We should be like the Bereans described in Acts 17:11:

Now the Bereans were of more noble character than the Thessalonians, for they received the message with great eagerness and examined the Scriptures every day to see if what Paul said was true.

Therefore, let us diligently examine the Scriptures to seek truth. Let us remember that the Lord even tells us what we should do when we see the blatant signs of the times indicating His soon return. In Luke 21:25-28, it is written:

There will be signs in the sun, moon and stars. On the earth, nations will be in anguish and perplexity at the roaring and tossing of the sea. Men will faint from terror, apprehensive of what is coming on the world, for the heavenly bodies will be shaken. At that time they will see the Son of Man coming in a cloud with power and great glory. When these things begin to take place, *stand up and lift up your heads*, because your redemption is drawing near (emphasis added).

The Old Testament even predicts the increase in the understanding of the signs of the times as the day of the Lord draws near. In Daniel 12:1-10 (NKJV), it is written:

At that time Michael shall stand up, the great prince who stands watch over the sons of your people; and there shall be a time of trouble, such as never was since there was a nation, even to that time. And at that time your people shall be delivered, every one who is found written in the book. And many of those who sleep in the dust of the earth shall awake, some to everlasting life, some to shame and everlasting contempt. Those who are wise shall shine like the brightness of the firmament, and those who turn many to righteousness like the stars forever and ever. But you, Daniel, shut up the words, and seal the book until the time of the end; many shall run to and fro, and knowledge shall increase.

Then I, Daniel, looked; and there stood two others, one on this riverbank and the other on that riverbank. And one said to the man clothed in linen, who was above the waters of the river, "How long shall the fulfillment of these wonders be?"

Then I heard the man clothed in linen, who was above the waters of the river, when he held up his right hand and his left hand to heaven, and swore by Him who lives forever, that it shall be for a time, times, and half a time; and when the power of the holy people has been completely shattered, all these things shall be finished.

Although I heard, I did not understand. Then I said, "My lord, what shall be the end of these things?"

And he said, "Go your way, Daniel, for the words are closed up and sealed till the time of the end. Many shall be purified, made white, and refined, but the wicked shall do wickedly; and none of the wicked shall understand, but *the wise shall understand*" (emphasis added).

Therefore, let us examine some of the signs in our day, while behaving like the Bereans and diligently examining Scripture as a standard for truth.

V. The Signs of Nature

Consider this reading from Matthew 24:1-8 (NASB):

Jesus came out from the temple and was going away when His disciples came up to point out the temple buildings to Him. And He said to them, "Do you not see all these things? Truly I say to you, not one stone here will be left upon another, which will not be torn down." As He was sitting on the Mount of Olives, the disciples came to Him privately, saying, "Tell us, when will these things happen, and what will be the sign of Your coming, and of the end of the age?" And Jesus answered and said to them, "See to it that no one misleads you. For many will come in My name, saying, 'I am the Christ,' and will mislead many. You will be hearing of wars and rumors of wars. See that you are not frightened, for those things must take place, but that is not yet the end. For nation will rise against nation, and kingdom against kingdom, and in various places there will be famines and earthquakes. But all these things are merely the beginning of birth pangs."

Ask any woman who has ever borne a child about birth pains and what happens over the time before delivery. She will tell you that birth pains increase in two things: frequency and intensity. Luke 21 parallels Matthew 24. In Luke 21:25, we see that Jesus also said "There will be signs in the sun, moon and stars. On the earth, nations will be in anguish and perplexity at the roaring and tossing of the sea."

Let's consider natural events like storms, earthquakes, plagues, and tidal waves. The 2005 Atlantic hurricane season saw twenty-eight tropical storms, making it the most active season on record.[46] It also saw fifteen hurricanes, the most hurricanes to form in a single season. Of those, seven became major hurricanes, one short of the 1950 season's record.[47]

The 2005 hurricane season was the first, Atlantic or Pacific, to exhaust the list of names and resort to Greek letters for naming.[48] The season caused massive damage, death, and destruction. The season caused well over $70 billion in damage (mostly from Hurricane Katrina) and over 2,800 deaths (mostly from Hurricane Katrina and Hurricane Stan).

The total number of tornadoes reported in the United States reached a record high in 2004. That year surpassed the previous record by almost three hundred tornadoes, according to a December 2004 press release issued by National Oceanic & Atmospheric Administration.[49]

The December 26, 2004, Indian Ocean earthquake was estimated to have a magnitude from between 9.0 to 9.3. It was one of the largest earthquakes ever recorded on a seismograph. The tsunami generated by the earthquake killed more people than any other natural disaster in history.[50]

The quake released an amount of energy equal to a 100-gigaton nuclear bomb, and that power lasted longer than any quake ever recorded. Normally, a small earthquake might last less than a second. A moderately sized earthquake might last a few seconds. This earthquake lasted about ten minutes. The quake, centered in the Indian Ocean, also created the biggest gash in the Earth's seabed ever observed, nearly eight hundred miles long. That is as long as a drive from Los Angeles, California, to Portland, Oregon.[51]

On October 8, 2005, an earthquake estimated to be 7.6 on the Richter scale struck at the India-Pakistan border and claimed over seventy-three thousand lives.[52]

In 2004, the World Health Organization estimated that, worldwide, between 2.8 and 3.5 million people died of AIDS. Since the first appearance of the disease in 1981, nineteen million people are estimated to have died from it. Many people also died in China in 2003 from the SARS epidemic. The latest world wide concern is Avian Flu.

Like birth pains, we see famines, earthquakes, and plagues increasing in intensity and frequency, just as Jesus told us.

VI. The Signs in Society

Jesus said that there will be "wars and rumors of wars" (Matt. 24:6). Let's look at the vast multitudes of people who died in wars or under oppressive governments in the last century.

Fifty million people are estimated to have died in World War II. Over Forty Eight million are estimated to have died under China's brutal government under Mao Zedong. Twenty million are estimated to have died in the former Soviet Union under Stalin. About fifteen million people died in World

War I. In the recent Second Sudanese Civil War, 1.9 million people are estimated to have died; 1.7 million are estimated to have died in the recent Congolese Civil War; 1.65 million people are estimated to have died under Cambodia's Khmer Rouge regime.[53]

Paul told Timothy in 2 Timothy 3:1-5:

> But mark this: There will be terrible times in the last days. People will be lovers of themselves, lovers of money, boastful, proud, abusive, disobedient to their parents, ungrateful, unholy, without love, unforgiving, slanderous, without self-control, brutal, not lovers of the good, treacherous, rash, conceited, lovers of pleasure rather than lovers of God— having a form of godliness but denying its power. Have nothing to do with them.

On October 27, 2005, two teenagers who believed police were chasing them were accidentally electrocuted in an area in France that is home to large populations of Muslim immigrants. A wave of violence followed. Small youth gangs roaming Paris' suburbs set fire to hundreds and hundreds of vehicles and attacked police and rescue workers.

A savage assault on a bus passenger illustrates how ruthless the rioters were. A bus had been forced to stop because of burning objects in its path. As a woman in her fifties on crutches tried to get off the bus, attackers doused her with an inflammable liquid and set her on fire. She was rescued by the driver and hospitalized with severe burns.[54]

This type of brutal, ruthless ultra-violence has become all too common over the world. In the Paris rioting that occurred over several days, more than nine thousand cars were burned.[55]

We also see a dramatic decline in personal morality. Let's take a snapshot of how quickly the decline came about during and after the sexual revolution of the 60s. In 1965, 69 percent of American women and 65 percent of men under the age of thirty said that premarital sex was always or almost always wrong. By 1972, those figures had plummeted to 24 percent of women and 21 percent of men. For women over the age of thirty, the figures dropped from 91 percent to 62 percent, and for men over the age of thirty from 62 percent to 47 percent: this in seven short years.[56]

Currently, over ten billion dollars is spent on pornography annually in this county. This is larger than the budgets of the NFL, NBA, and Major League Baseball combined. There are over 2 million known porn sites on the Internet, and more than 2,500 new sites coming online every week.[57]

In 2002, nine out of ten children aged between eight and sixteen had viewed pornography on the Internet.[58] In a 2000 study, twenty-five million Americans visited cyber-sex sites between one and ten hours per week. Another 4.7 million indulged in excess of eleven hours per week.[59]

In a 2001 study, 51 percent of pastors surveyed said cyber porn was a possible temptation; 37 percent said it was a current struggle.[60] In a 2000 Focus on the Family bulletin, it was reported that 63 percent of men attending "Men, Romance, & Integrity Seminars" admitted to struggling with porn in the past year. Two-thirds are in church leadership and one-tenth are pastors.[61] One in seven calls to Focus on the Family's Pastoral Care Line is about Internet pornography.[62] These figures have certainly increased over time.

We are likewise seeing a dramatic decline in the sanctity of the family.

Throughout most of this nation's history, we have revered and cherished the family. In an 1888 case, the U.S. Supreme Court characterized marriage as "the most important relation in life," and as "the foundation of the family and of society, without which there would be neither civilization nor progress."[63] In a 1923 case, the court recognized that the right "to marry, establish a home and bring up children" is a central part of the liberty protected by the due process clause of the Constitution.[64] In another Supreme Court case in 1942, the court said "marriage and procreation are fundamental to the very existence and survival of the race."[65]

In the past few decades, the institution of marriage has been under attack. In 1970, one out of ten families in the U.S. was headed by a single parent. In 1990, three out of ten were. More than half of all marriages end in divorce, often leaving wrecked lives, mountains of debt, and permanently scarred children in their wake.[66]

Regrettably, the rate of divorce among professing Christians is about the same as what it is for the rest of society.[67] We have become a nation that "looks out for number one." We justify our selfishness. Jesus told us, "Love your neighbor as yourself." He never told us and, indeed, never had to tell us to love ourselves. We do that already quite well.

Psychologists, economists, and sociologists are finally acknowledging that divorce is far more harmful than we used to think. It makes everyone poorer, especially women and children. Children of divorce are twice as likely to be abused and to get in trouble with the law or to become teen moms, even if they have step-parents. And divorce doesn't end fighting in front of the children; in most cases, it escalates it! Consider these facts about divorce cited in a 2003 *National Review* article[68]:

> In America, divorce used to be difficult to obtain and, usually, impossible without good reason: adultery, abandonment, abuse, alcoholism. In 1880, according to the historian Robert L. Griswold, one marriage in 21—fewer than 5 percent—ended in divorce. Over time, there have been peaks and valleys in the divorce rate, such as the period immediately following World

War II, when returning soldiers found things rather different from how they had left them, or were themselves tremendously changed by war. "But beginning in the mid-1960s," writes Griswold, the divorce rate "again began to rise dramatically, fueled by ever-higher marital expectations, a vast expansion of wives moving into the work force, the rebirth of feminism, and the adoption of 'no fault' divorce (that is, divorce granted without the need to establish wrongdoing by either party) in almost every state." Griswold continues, "The last factor, although hailed as a progressive step that would end the fraud, collusion, and acrimony that accompanied the adversarial system of divorce, has had disastrous consequences for women and children."

While about half of all marriages end in divorce, the Bible says "Marriage should be honored by all, and the marriage bed kept pure, for God will judge the adulterer and all the sexually immoral" (Heb. 13:4). In Malachi 2:13-16, it is written:

"I hate divorce," says the LORD God of Israel, "and I hate a man's covering his wife with violence as well as with his garment," says the LORD Almighty. So guard yourself in your spirit, and do not break faith.

VII. Spiritual Signs in the Crumbling Church

The Christian church in this country as a whole has become compromised. All across this nation, you can find churches that look like the Laodicean church described in Revelation 3.

In today's church, there are many more false converts, that is, people who think they are Christian but who really are not. They have never established a personal relationship with God through faith in Jesus Christ. They attend church faithfully and may even occupy prominent leadership positions within the church. Jesus warned us about wolves in sheep's clothing, and He told us that "by their fruits ye shall know them" (Matt. 7:20 KJV).

Such people have never been born again. They have not been born of the Spirit, which is imperative. Jesus said it very plainly in John 3:1-6:

> Now there was a man of the Pharisees named Nicodemus, a member of the Jewish ruling council. He came to Jesus at night and said, "Rabbi, we know you are a teacher who has come from God. For no one could perform the miraculous signs you are doing if God were not with him." In reply Jesus declared, "I tell you the truth, no one can see the kingdom of God unless he is born again." "How can a man be born when he is old?" Nicodemus asked. "Surely he cannot enter a second time into his mother's womb to be born!" Jesus answered, "I tell you the truth, no one can enter the kingdom of God unless he is born of water and the Spirit. Flesh gives birth to flesh, but the Spirit gives birth to spirit. You should not be surprised at my saying, 'You must be born again.' The wind blows wherever it pleases. You hear its sound, but you cannot tell where it comes from or where it is going. So it is with everyone born of the Spirit."

On at least two occasions in the Bible, Paul speaks of "false brethren." We see them throughout the church today. They are people who are more interested in attending church to impress people than to worship God. They are friends of the world. In James 4:4-5, it is written, "You adulterous people, don't you know that friendship with the world is hatred toward God? Anyone who chooses to be a friend of the world becomes an enemy of God. Or do you think Scripture says without reason that the spirit he caused to live in us envies intensely?"

In many pulpits across this country, a name-it-and-claim-it, happy-clappy, prosperity gospel is preached. These preachers promise success and an easy life. They falsely teach people that if you are suffering, you must not be right with God. This is heresy. Paul wrote to Timothy, "Those who want to lead godly lives in Christ Jesus will suffer persecution" (2 Tim. 3:12). The happy clappy, name-it-and-claim-it, prosperity gospel that is preached in this country is an affront to our brothers and sisters who suffer severe persecution in places like North Korea, China, Indonesia, Pakistan, Bangladesh, and a host of Middle Eastern countries.

Elsewhere in the world, our fellow brethren are often in fear for their lives just because of what they believe. The increase of apostasy in the church (that is, corrupt doctrine) should not surprise us, for the Bible very clearly teaches that there will be a falling away (apostasy) preceding the Lord. Paul wrote, in 2 Thessalonians 2:1-4 (NKJV):

> Now, brethren, concerning the coming of our Lord Jesus Christ and our gathering together to Him, we ask you, not to be soon shaken in mind or troubled, either by spirit or by word or by letter, as if from us, as though the day of Christ had come. Let no one deceive you by any means; for that Day will not come unless the *falling away comes first*, and the man of sin is revealed, the son of perdition, who opposes and exalts himself above all that is called God or that is worshiped, so that he sits as God in the temple of God, showing himself that he is God (emphasis added).

The Bible is clear that many people will die expecting heaven yet receiving hell. Jesus said in Matthew 7:21-23:

> Not everyone who says to me, "Lord, Lord," will enter the kingdom of heaven, but only he who does the will of my Father who is in heaven. Many will say to me on that day, "Lord, Lord, did we not prophesy in your name, and in your name drive out demons and perform many miracles?" Then I will tell them plainly, "I never knew you. Away from me, you evildoers!"

The increase in false converts is tied to the decline among those who profess to be Christians in the essential beliefs which are part of real Christianity. This decline in belief in essential tenets of Christianity, in turn, has its roots in the growing disbelief that the Bible is true.

John Wesley, a prominent Christian who lived about three hundred years ago, once said of the Bible "if there be any mistakes in the Bible there may as well be a thousand. If there be one falsehood in that book it did not come from the God of truth."[69] To believe that there is error in the Bible leads down the slippery slope into moral relevancy. That is because if the Bible were not true, or even if it were partially untrue, we could never know what pleases God or what angers God.

Yet, we believers know that the Bible in its original text is true, and we know that God controlled the men who wrote it. In the book of Acts, when Luke described the storm that shipwrecked him and Paul, he wrote:

> On the fourteenth night we were still being driven across the Adriatic Sea, when about midnight the sailors sensed they were approaching land.
>
> Acts 27:27

The Greek word translated "driven" here is *pheromai*. It is the same Greek word that is translated as "carried along" in 1 Peter 1:19-21:

> And we have the word of the prophets made more certain, and you will do well to pay attention to it, as to a light shining in a dark place, until the day dawns and the morning star rises in your hearts. Above all, you must understand that no prophecy of Scripture came about by the prophet's own interpretation. For prophecy never had its origin in the will of man, but men spoke from God as they were carried along by the Holy Spirit.

If you consider the apostles' ship that was shipwrecked in Acts 27, you understand that it was driven by an overwhelming wind and the captain of that ship could not control its destination. As it was being driven along, it never stopped being a ship (that is, of course, until it crashed).

In the same way, the Holy Spirit carried along (*pheromai*) the men who wrote down what became known as the Holy Bible. It was not of their own minds or thinking that they wrote, but they were driven by the Holy Spirit.

They did not cease to be men, but they were totally controlled by the Holy Spirit (in that sense, they were incapable of resisting the Spirit) when writing the text of the Bible. Indeed, they may not have understood at the time that it was the Spirit driving them, but they, just like the ship described in Acts 27, were totally controlled by a force that they could not resist.

We should always remember that Satan does not want us to believe or understand God's Word. Think about it. What were the first words that Satan ever spoke to mankind? "Did God really say? (Gen. 3:1). Satan wants us to doubt God's Word and meaning, yet we know God's Word to be true.

A 2001 survey of what Americans believe conducted by the Barna Research Group revealed that most people in this country who profess to be Christian do not believe in some of the basic, essential tenets of faith.[70] A United Press International article entitled "Poll shows Protestant collapse" that cited the survey observed:[71]

For example, a mere 21 percent of America's Lutherans, 20 percent of the Episcopalians, 18 percent of Methodists, and 22 percent of Presbyterians affirm the basic Protestant tenet that by good works man does not earn his way to heaven.

Yet the doctrine that man is justified before God alone by grace through faith in Christ's saving work (and that good works are simply the fruits of faith) is the very foundation of the 16th century Reformation. It is a theological principle the Vatican, too, has accepted in its 1999 accord with the Lutheran World Federation.

But the Barna poll discloses that only 9 percent of the Catholics in the United States agree with this theological concept that Martin Luther had culled from chapter 3 of the apostle Paul's epistle to the Romans.

The article quotes Gerald McDermott, an Episcopalian, as saying, "This happened because in the last 30 years American pastors have lost their nerve to preach a theology that goes against the grain of American narcissism. What we are witnessing now is what (evangelicalism's premier thinker) Francis Shaeffer predicted over 20 years ago — that the

American church of the future would be dedicated solely to peace and affluence."

Do you hear what McDermott is saying? The modern church has become anemic largely because of unbiblical teaching from the pulpits.

The Barna survey also revealed that "only 33 percent of the American Catholics, Lutherans and Methodists, and 28 percent of the Episcopalians agreed with the statement that Christ was without sin."[72]

What is astounding is Americans' disbelief in Satan: "While most of the sample American queried by Barna still affirmed God as the all-powerful Creator, a mere 17 percent of the Catholics, 18 percent Methodists, 20 percent Episcopalians, 21 percent Lutherans, and 22 percent of the Presbyterians told Barna that they thought Satan was real."[73]

VIII. Signs in Technology

The United States currently has in excess of ten thousand nuclear warheads. Worldwide, there are roughly thirty thousand nuclear warheads, and about seventeen thousand five hundred are considered operational.[74]

In 2002, North Korea admitted to having a program to enrich uranium for use in nuclear weapons. With its admission, North Korea breached the Agreed Framework signed in 1994 with United States, under which the North Koreans agreed to freeze their nuclear weapons program. North Korea declared its possession of a nuclear deterrent on February 10, 2005.[75]

On September 7, 1997, the CBS newsmagazine Sixty Minutes broadcasted an alarming story in which former Russian National Security Adviser Aleksandr Lebed claimed that the Russian military had lost track of more than one hundred suitcase-sized nuclear bombs. These smaller bombs can kill up to one hundred thousand people. Lebed stated that these devices were made to look like suitcases, and could be detonated by one person within half an hour.[76]

Pyotr Simonenko, the leader of the Ukrainian Communist Party, released a sensational statement on September 11, 2002. In his words, there were formerly two thousand four hundred nuclear warheads in Ukraine, although the transport of only two thousand two hundred of them back to Russia was officially documented. Simonenko claimed that nobody knows where the other two hundred Soviet-era nukes from the Ukraine are.[77]

Our minds cannot fathom how bad it will be if there is a global thermonuclear war. With the massive proliferation of nuclear warheads, particularly given the numbers that are unaccounted for and may be in the hands of terrorists, it appears that a nuclear holocaust is likely.

When that happens, the earth will likely be consumed by fire. This is consistent with what is written in the Bible. Consider 2 Peter 3:9-13:

> The Lord is not slow in keeping his promise, as some understand slowness. He is patient with you, not wanting anyone to perish, but everyone to come to repentance. But the day of the Lord will come like a thief. The heavens will disappear with a roar; the elements will be destroyed by fire, and the earth and everything in it will be laid bare. Since everything will be destroyed in this way, what kind of people ought you to be? You ought to live holy and godly lives as you look forward to the day of God and speed its coming. That day will bring about the destruction of the heavens by fire, and the elements will melt in the heat. But in keeping with his promise we are looking forward to a new heaven and a new earth, the home of righteousness.

And also consider Zechariah 14:12:

This is the plague with which the LORD will strike all the nations that fought against Jerusalem: Their flesh will rot while they are still standing on their feet, their eyes will rot in their sockets, and their tongues will rot in their mouths.

Friends, these types of apocalyptic happenings are easily understandable in light of how horrifically we can destroy each other with modern technology.

IX. The Signs in Israel

One of the most significant signs of the times is the nation Israel itself. In Mark 11:12-14, Jesus cursed a fig tree that bore no fruit. This cursing was symbolic of the impending uprooting of the nation of Israel. The temple in Jerusalem was destroyed by the Romans in 70 A.D., and the slaughter of the Jews was terrible.

This event opened and ushered in the time of the Gentiles, which has been going on for nearly two thousand years. But God has not finished with Israel. He still loves Israel, and the apostle Paul fully explains this in Romans 9-11. Indeed, Paul wrote in Romans 11:25:

I do not want you to be ignorant of this mystery, brothers, so that you may not be conceited: Israel has experienced a hardening in part until the full number of the Gentiles has come in.

Jesus also used a fig tree analogy to conclude his lengthy discourse in Matthew 24, when He spoke of signs of the times and His soon return. Jesus said in Matthew 24:32-33:

Now learn this lesson from the fig tree: As soon as its twigs get tender and its leaves come out, you know that summer is near. Even so, when you see all these things, you know that it is near, right at the door.

Thus, the fig tree also symbolizes Israel and its rebirth and recent restoration with prosperity. Most of us are too young to remember the significance of the event, but on May 14, 1948, something happened that has never happened before. An ancient nation that was extinct became revived: Israel was reborn.

God orchestrated this rebirth largely through the two World Wars. At the end of World War I, God liberated the ancient land of Israel from over four hundred years of dominion by the Ottoman Turks, and the land became a British Protectorate. You may remember that the Turks had sided with the Germans, the ultimate losers in World War I.

Interestingly, once the ancient land of Israel was back in the hands of Jewish allies after World War I, not many Jews returned to the land. After the fierce and horrific persecution that the Jews suffered in World War II, however, they came in droves and wanted to establish their own homeland. Through the events of World War I, God prepared the land for the Jewish people, and through the events of World War II, God prepared the Jewish people for the land.

The Bible is very clear in many places that before the Lord comes again, He will regather Jews to Israel and the temple will be rebuilt. In Ezekiel 36:24, God said, "For I will take you out of the nations; I will gather you from all the countries and bring you back into your own land." (See also, Isa. 11:10-12, Ezek. 37:1-12, Zech. 10:6-12, Isa. 52:1-10, and Zech. 12:3,6.)

One hundred years ago, there were practically no signs at all that we were approaching the end times. Now there are so many signs that it is hard to keep track of them all.

Let's look at what happened during World War I that hailed the soon return of Jesus. In the early 1900s, there lived a Russian Jew named Dr. Chaim Weizmann, who served as a chemistry professor in England at the University of Manchester. He was also a leader of a committee of Zionists who were seeking a homeland for the Jews.

He was very politically minded. He made friends with many British leaders who also happened to be very familiar with Bible prophecy and were sympathetic to the Jewish desire to return to their homeland, which was then called Palestine.

Weizmann was very popular among the British government. As a chemist, he invented a method of producing synthetic acetone, a chemical that had been in short supply and that was an ingredient necessary for the production of the naval explosive cordite.[78]

Weizmann lobbied the British government for a British Protectorate over a Jewish homeland. He was well received. This effort ultimately resulted in the issuance of the Balfour declaration written on November 2, 1917, by Arthur Balfour to Lord Rothschild, president of the British Zionist Federation. Note carefully what the declaration contains:

> I have much pleasure in conveying to you, on behalf of His Majesty's Government, the following declaration of sympathy with Jewish Zionist aspirations which has been submitted to, and approved by, the Cabinet.
>
> His Majesty's Government view with favour the establishment in Palestine of a national home for the Jewish people, and will use their best efforts to facilitate the achievement of this object, it being clearly understood that nothing shall be done which may prejudice the rights of existing non-Jewish

communities in Palestine, or the rights and political status of Jews in any other country.

I should be grateful if you would bring this declaration to the knowledge of the Zionist Federation.[79]

What is absolutely amazing about this proclamation is that it was issued nearly a year before World War I officially ended on November 11, 1918. The British were promising land to the Jews that at the time belonged to the Ottoman Empire! This is one of the first major signs of the Lord Jesus' soon return.

On December 11, 1917, the city of Jerusalem was liberated by the British from four hundred years of Turkish rule. The British troops were led by British General Edmund Allenby, who was himself a devout Christian. When he entered the city, he refused to ride his horse. He walked in because the Scriptures say that the Messiah is the one who will enter Jerusalem on a white horse at the time of His second coming (Rev. 19:11).

Interestingly, the Arab world initially looked on Allenby's capture of Jerusalem as a matter of divine intervention. This was due to the mistaken belief that Allenby's name was a combination of their words *Allah* (meaning "God" to the Arabs) and *Neby* (meaning "prophet").[80]

As soon as Israel declared her independence on May 14, 1948, she was immediately attacked by all the surrounding Arab countries. Yet God's purpose prevailed and she survived. The land has been a hotbed of controversy ever since. Muslims claim the land and want the land for themselves. Many outspoken Muslim leaders have publicly called for the extermination of Israel. But consider this: Jerusalem has never been the capital of any Arab or Muslim state. Jerusalem is mentioned 667 times in the Hebrew Scriptures, 144 times in the New Testament, but not once in the Koran.

God looks after Israel. This tiny nation survived the 1948 War for Independence, the 1956 Sinai Campaign, the 1967 Six Day War (during which the Jews re-occupied Jerusalem on June 7, 1967), the 1973 Yom Kippur war, and numerous lesser conflicts ever since.

The Bible says that God will bless those who bless Israel, and He will curse those who curse Israel (Gen. 12:3). The Bible also says that he who touches Israel touches "the apple of God's eye" (Zech. 2:8).

Now, let's look at what our government in United States has done to Israel and see how those actions tie in with signs of the times. Let's look specifically at the policies of our current and past two administrations.

An Aside

I will not tell you whether or not I like President Bush, former President Clinton, or the older President Bush. It does not matter whether I like them or not. I have a Christian duty to pray for them. It is written in 1 Tim. 2:1-4:

> *urge, then, first of all, that requests, prayers, inter-cession and thanksgiving be made for everyone— for kings and all those in authority, that we may live peaceful and quiet lives in all godliness and holiness. This is good, and pleases God our Savior, who wants all men to be saved and to come to a knowledge of the truth.*

I should pray for them and you should pray for them. Many Christians greatly dishonored our Lord by their bitter and sarcastic mockery of former President Clinton when they should have been praying for him. Do you understand, friends, that not only should you pray for our leaders in government, but that you should also pray for

*your warden and the guards over you? We have a Christian
duty to do so.*

A *Lamplighter* magazine article entitled "Hurricane
Katrina: The Prophetic Significance" written by Dr. Dave
Reagan draws some absolutely amazing connections between
"U.S. mistreatment of Israel and subsequent natural calami-
ties, economic setbacks and political crises"[81] (the article
draws from a more comprehensive work in the book *Eye
to Eye* by William Koenig, a White House correspondent).
Consider what Dr. Reagan says was the turning point:

> The turning point was in 1991 when the Soviet
> Union collapsed and Russian Jews began flooding
> into Israel at the rate of 2,000 to 3,000 a day for one
> year. The tiny nation of Israel was overwhelmed by
> the refugees. The Israeli government appealed to the
> World Bank for a $5 billion loan. The bank said it
> would grant the loan only if the U. S. guaranteed it.
> The Bush Administration agreed to underwrite the
> loan on one condition: the Israelis had to go to the
> bargaining table and start trading land for peace.[82]

The article continues with a comprehensive review of
our nation's attitude towards Israel over the past decade and
a half. It also reveals that our nation has always suffered
terrible disasters (coincidentally?) any time we have been
domineering towards Israel. Let's consider some of the more
prominent events that Dr. Reagan detailed:

*__The Madrid Conference__ — This conference, which
we forced on Israel, marked the beginning of the "land
for peace" process. The opening of the conference on
October 30, 1991, coincided with the formation of
"the Perfect Storm." This was the record breaking*

*storm along our Atlantic seacoast which produced 100 foot high waves and heavily damaged President Bush's home at Kennebunkport, Maine. The headlines of **USA Today** on November 1, 1991, had the stories of the storm and the Madrid Conference side by side.*

*<u>**Round Six of the Bilateral Peace Talks**</u> — In June of 1992 Yitzhak Rabin was elected the new Prime Minister of Israel. We immediately insisted that he come to Washington, D.C. and meet with Yasser Arafat. The day that meeting began, August 24, 1992, Hurricane Andrew slammed into Florida with winds of 177 miles per hour. The damage done amounted to over $30 billion — the most costly hurricane in U.S. History to that point in time.*

*<u>**Arafat at the United Nations**</u> — In September of 1998 Yasser Arafat was invited to speak to a special session of the United Nations that was held in New York. President Clinton arranged a meeting with him to put pressure on Israel. As the meeting took place, Hurricane Georges smashed into the Gulf Coast causing over $6 billion in damage.*

*<u>**Arafat and a Palestinian State**</u> — With our encouragement, Arafat announced that he was going to proclaim a Palestinian state on May 4, 1999. Even though President Clinton later persuaded Arafat to postpone the declaration to at least December, on the very day the proclamation was to have been made (May 3rd in the U.S.; May 4th in Israel), the most powerful tornado in U.S. history tore through Oklahoma City with wind speeds of 316 miles per hour, destroying over 2,000 homes.*

__The Camp David Summit__ — From July 11 through July 24 in the summer of 2000, President Clinton hosted a summit conference between Israel and the Palestinian Authority. Clinton pressured Israeli Prime Minister Ehud Barak to surrender the heartland of Israel. During these precise dates, a major heat wave struck the South Central U.S. and fires broke out in our Western states. At one point, there were over 50 active fires that consumed over 500,000 acres before the end of the month.

__White House Ramadan Celebration__ — On Thursday evening, November 7, 2002, President Bush hosted a dinner at the White House to honor the Muslim religious holiday called Ramadan. In his speech that evening, the President said:

. . . this season commemorates the revelation of God's word in the holy Koran to the prophet Muhammad. Today this word inspires faithful Muslims to lead lives of honesty and integrity and compassion . . .

We see in Islam a religion that traces its origins back to God's call on Abraham . . .

Two days later a total of 88 tornados hit Arkansas, Tennessee, Alabama, Mississippi, Georgia, Ohio, and Pennsylvania..

__The Middle East Peace Plan__ — On April 30, 2003, U.S. Ambassador Daniel Kurtzer presented the "Road Map" peace plan to Israeli Prime Minister Ariel Sharon. It was a plan formulated by an ungodly coalition called "the Quartet." This group was made up of Russia, the European Union, the United Nations, *and the United States. It called for Israel to surrender Gaza and its heartland of Judea and Samaria to the Palestinians. On May 3rd Secretary of State Colin Powell departed for the Middle East for talks to implement the plan. On May 4th Secretary Powell met with terrorist leader Hafez Assad of Syria and made a commitment to him to include the surrender of the Golan Heights in the peace plan. That day a swarm of tornados began tearing apart the Central United States. Over the next 7 days, there was a total of 412 tornados — the largest cluster ever observed by NOAA since it began its record keeping in 1950. The previous record had been 177 in 1999.*

In summary, between October 1991 and November 2004, the United States experienced:

- *9 of the 10 largest insurance events in U.S. history.*

- *9 of the 10 greatest natural disasters as ranked by FEMA relief costs.*

- *5 of the costliest hurricanes in U.S. history*

- *3 of the 4 largest tornado swarms in U.S. history.*

All of which were linked to our attempts to pressure Israel into either dividing up its land or surrendering part of its capital city of Jerusalem.[83]

The last week of January 2003 saw Ariel Sharon over-whelmingly re-elected as Israeli prime minister in spite of

the fact that he ignored the views of many of his constitu-
ents against the creation of a Palestinian state. That same
week saw President Bush's State of the Union Address. Right
after that, on February 1, 2003, the Space Shuttle Columbia
disintegrated in the sky over President Bush's home state,
not far from his Crawford, Texas, ranch. The first debris was
sighted in Palestine, Texas. Six Americans and the first Israeli
astronaut were aboard. This event seems to have a profound
symbolism...deaths of Americans and Israelis over Palestine.

All of these can be linked to our attempts to pressure
Israel into either dividing up its land or surrendering part
of its capital city of Jerusalem. Is this any wonder when we
consider what God said in Joel 3:2?

> I will gather all nations and bring them down to the
> Valley of Jehoshaphat. There I will enter into judg-
> ment against them concerning my inheritance, my
> people Israel, for they scattered my people among the
> nations and *divided up my land* (emphasis added).

The parallels between the United States' treatment of
Israel become even more fascinating when you consider
what happened when the withdrawal ended. Here's another
excerpt from Dr. Reagan's article:

> *The Gaza Withdrawal*— *The most recent chaotic
> event in Israel was the forced withdrawal of all Jews
> from Gaza. It began on August 7th and continued
> through the 22nd, as nearly 9,000 Israelis were
> uprooted from their land and homes. Many had been
> in the area for as long as 35 years.*
>
> *It was a heart-wrenching event to watch women and
> children manhandled, synagogues violated, torah
> scrolls desecrated, houses bulldozed, graves dug*

up, and farms destroyed. Entire Jewish communities were forcibly removed from land which God has given to the Jewish people as an everlasting possession (Psalm 105:8-11).

The economic impact on the Israeli economy will be overwhelming. The farms in Gaza represented 70% of Israel's organic produce, 60% of the nation's exported herbs, 15% of its total agricultural exports, 60% of its exported cherry tomato crop, and $120 million of its flower exports.

And while this travesty was taking place, Secretary of State Condoleezza Rice began applying more pressure with the following statement: "Everyone empathizes with what the Israelis are facing . . . but it cannot be Gaza only."

The Supernatural Response — The withdrawal ended on August 22nd, and on the very next day, the government of Bermuda announced that a tropical depression had formed off its coast. Dubbed "Katrina," the storm quickly developed into the most powerful hurricane in modern history. It slammed into New Orleans and the Mississippi coast four days later on the 27th. The hurricane disrupted 25% of our crude oil production and destroyed our nation's largest port (the 5th largest in the world in terms of tonnage).[84]

On November 15, 2005, Condoleezza Rice was in Israel and strong-armed Israel to yield control of the Egypt/Gaza Strip border to Palestinians. The next day, the American Midwest was ravaged by tornadoes.[85]

Another Aside

I would be remiss if I did not remind the reader that we ought not to hate the Muslim, but we ought to love him. God did not call us to destroy those who do believe as we do, but to show them the love of God in Jesus Christ. It is written in Luke 9:51-56 (NKJV):

Now it came to pass, when the time had come for Him to be received up, that He steadfastly set His face to go to Jerusalem, and sent messengers before His face. And as they went, they entered a village of the Samaritans, to prepare for Him. But they did not receive Him, because His face was set for the journey to Jerusalem. And when His disciples James and John saw this, they said, "Lord, do You want us to command fire to come down from heaven and consume them, just as Elijah did?" But He turned and rebuked them, and said, "You do not know what manner of spirit you are of. For the Son of Man did not come to destroy men's lives but to save them." And they went to another village.

Thus, just as we pray for the Jew, we should pray for the Muslim. God desires all men and women to come to repentance. "Do I take any pleasure in the death of the wicked? declares the Sovereign LORD. Rather, am I not pleased when they turn from their ways and live?" (Ezek. 18:23). We have a Christian duty to pray for those who do not believe as we do.

God has overwhelmingly blessed this nation, largely because of our godly heritage and godly roots. Yet His Word says that to whom much is given, much is expected (Luke 12:47-48). The Lord also disciplines those He loves (Heb.

12:7). We, as a nation, are turning our back on the Lord. I fear for this nation. It is a scary thing to be disciplined by almighty God. We are seeing Psalm 2:1-6 played out right before our eyes in living color:

> Why do the nations conspire and the peoples plot in vain? The kings of the earth take their stand and the rulers gather together against the LORD and against his Anointed One. "Let us break their chains," they say, "and throw off their fetters." The One enthroned in heaven laughs; the Lord scoffs at them. Then he rebukes them in his anger and terrifies them in his wrath, saying, "I have installed my King on Zion, my holy hill."

Yet the secular world ridicules us believers, and they scoff at the thought of Jesus' second coming. The Bible also predicted the scoffers in 2 Peter 3:1-7:

> Dear friends, this is now my second letter to you. I have written both of them as reminders to stimulate you to wholesome thinking. I want you to recall the words spoken in the past by the holy prophets and the command given by our Lord and Savior through your apostles. First of all, you must understand that in the last days scoffers will come, scoffing and following their own evil desires. They will say, "Where is this 'coming' he promised? Ever since our fathers died, everything goes on as it has since the beginning of creation." But they deliberately forget that long ago by God's word the heavens existed and the earth was formed out of water and by water. By these waters also the world of that time was deluged and destroyed. By the same word the present heavens and earth are

reserved for fire, being kept for the day of judgment and destruction of ungodly men.

X. Repent and Believe

What shall we do then in light of the impending, terrible judgment that is coming on the earth? A Southern Baptist international missionary who had survived numerous life threatening situations once said, "The safest place in the world is the center of God's will." Consider this text from Matthew 8:23-27 (NKJV):

Now when He got into a boat, His disciples followed Him. And suddenly a great tempest arose on the sea, so that the boat was covered with the waves. But He was asleep. Then His disciples came to Him and awoke Him, saying, "Lord, save us! We are perishing!"

But He said to them, "Why are you fearful, O you of little faith?" Then He arose and rebuked the winds and the sea, and there was a great calm. So the men marveled, saying, "Who can this be, that even the winds and the sea obey Him?"[86]

The Lord can save us in every calamity, whether it is fire, earthquake, tornado, hurricane, or personal disaster.

Sin so permeates our lives that it is like yeast kneaded into a loaf of bread. The Bible says that at the time of the great flood "the LORD saw how great man's wickedness on the earth had become, and that every inclination of the thoughts of his heart was only evil all the time" (Gen. 6:5). Elsewhere, it is written, "The heart is deceitful above all things and beyond cure. Who can understand it?" (Jer 17:9).

Ask most people, at least in this country, if they think they will go to heaven, and they will say, "Sure, I've lived a pretty good life." And they will tell you about the good things they have done and the bad things they have not done.

Consider again that three of the most prominent men in the Bible were murderers. Moses murdered an Egyptian. King David committed adultery with Bathsheba, his loyal friend Uriah's wife. When she became pregnant, David arranged to have Uriah killed so he could marry Bathsheba right away without anyone knowing about the adultery.

Finally, the apostle Paul twice admits that he was a persecutor of the church and that he stood by giving his approval when the Jews martyred Stephen. How great is the love of our Lord Jesus Christ! His grace and glory are magnified by how wretched a man He can save and redeem! The Lord turned the greatest enemy of the church into one of the greatest and most devoted apostles. All the evil things these men did were washed away by the blood of Jesus Christ. They were justified and made righteous by their faith in Jesus Christ.

We have to come to the Lord in humility, in complete surrender. Consider the man in Matthew 19:16-22:

> Now a man came up to Jesus and asked, "Teacher, what good thing must I do to get eternal life?" "Why do you ask me about what is good?" Jesus replied. "There is only One who is good. If you want to enter life, obey the commandments."
>
> "Which ones?" the man inquired. Jesus replied, "'Do not murder, do not commit adultery, do not steal, do not give false testimony, honor your father and mother,' and 'love your neighbor as yourself.'"
>
> "All these I have kept," the young man said. "What do I still lack?" Jesus answered, "If you want to be

perfect, go, sell your possessions and give to the poor, and you will have treasure in heaven. Then come, follow me."

When the young man heard this, he went away sad, because he had great wealth.

This man had the mindset of the world, and of all other religions besides pure Christianity. He asked, "What good things must I do?" The whole world thinks that if we do good, we will go to heaven.

The truth is, we know the difference between good and evil. We know what we should do, but we cannot do it. Jesus challenged the man with the law, that is, the Ten Commandments. The man was quite content with himself that he had obeyed all of the commandments.

With what did Jesus start when responding to this young man? The Lord started with those commandments to which obedience is obvious for all to see. All of the man's friends could attest that he honored his father and mother. But Jesus went further, because He sees the heart. When Jesus told the man what he still had to do, Jesus did not give the man a checklist of deeds (remember that we cannot do good). He told him to give up his idol, which was his wealth. The man could perhaps truthfully say that he had obeyed the commandments that govern how man deals with man, but his god was his money. He constantly violated the first and second commandments.

Friends, if I examine myself and you examine yourself in the light of the Ten Commandments, you and I can see that we deserve hell. We deserve God's earthly punishment. God says in Ezekiel 18:4, "For every living soul belongs to me, the father as well as the son—both alike belong to me. The soul who sins is the one who will die." So how do we escape this sentence of eternal death?

In John 5:24, Jesus said, "I tell you the truth, whoever hears my word and believes him who sent me has eternal life and will not be condemned; he has crossed over from death to life."

And again, we read, "Jesus did many other miraculous signs in the presence of his disciples, which are not recorded in this book. But these are written that you may believe that Jesus is the Christ, the Son of God, and that by believing you may have life in his name" (John 20:30-31). "If you confess with your mouth, 'Jesus is Lord,' and believe in your heart that God raised him from the dead, you will be saved" (Rom. 10:9). If you do not already know the Lord, repent and believe while there is still time. Fly from the coming wrath.

CHAPTER 11

Conclusion

—ᜀ—

Dear reader, now you know my passion. I love bringing the good news of Jesus Christ to people, especially to those who have no hope, like the inmates in prison. Yet this does not mean I have become some loopy liberal who thinks that all a person needs is a little more rehab to do better.

Nor does my passion mean that I have become soft in the administration of justice. "This is what the LORD Almighty says: 'Administer true justice; show mercy and compassion to one another'" (Zech. 7:9). I have a duty to seek true justice both as a matter of fulfilling my public office and as a matter of pleasing God. J.I. Packer, in his great work *Knowing God* said it well[87]:

> The modern idea that a judge should be cold and dispassionate has no place in the Bible. The biblical judge is expected to love justice and fair play and to loathe all ill treatment of one person by another. An unjust judge, one who has no interest in seeing right triumph over wrong, is by biblical standards a monstrosity. The Bible leaves us in no doubt that God loves righteousness and hates iniquity, and the

ideal of a judge wholly identified with what is good and right is perfectly fulfilled in him.

My passion has not made me naive either. Some inmates have chosen hell, and they will not retreat from that decision. Timothy McVeigh murdered 168 people. Right before he was executed, he quoted an old poem from 1875 by William Earnest Henley:

"It matters not how straight the gate, how charged with punishments the scroll, I am the captain of my fate, I am the master of my soul."

I expect that Timothy McVeigh sailed his soul right into the lake of fire. Yet, there are the Karla Faye Tuckers and others out there whom the Lord can save and change in spite of the horrifying nature of their crimes. While some cannot grasp the truth of the matter, the grace of God can save even the man described in chapter 1 whom I sent to prison for raping a seven-year-old girl.

There are about 152,000 inmates incarcerated in nearly 100 prisons in the State of Texas, and, Texas has approximately 767,765 people under the control of its Criminal Justice Correctional System (that is, the total number of people on probation, in county jails, in prison and on parole).[88] This is more than the population of some states.

Our society treats these people like human rubbish, disposable people who can be tossed on the trash heap of society. They are not disposable people. God loves them. We in the free world are just like them in our hearts. And God wants to save them. "The Lord is not slow in keeping his promise, as some understand slowness. He is patient with you, *not wanting anyone to perish*, but everyone to come to repentance" (2 Pet. 3:9, emphasis added).

It is my hope that I can continue to go into prison with the Good News. I would also be delighted if this little book got into the hands of a great number of inmates, but I cannot do this by myself.

I took a pay cut to become a judge, and as a provider for a family of eight on a judge's pay, there is only so much I can do. Yet, even if one or many benefactors came forward to buy copies of this book for the inmates, that is not what it is needed most.

What is needed most are godly women and men like Pat Howard and Dub Pearson to show the inmates the love of God in Jesus Christ. Do you remember that inmate named Brian (his letter is quoted in chapter 1) who wrote me and described the horrific things he endured as a child? Consider what Brian says about his life now:

> I have been through so much in my life to where I just grew to a very miserable and bitter man. And it's really sad when I think about how I spent my whole life in sorrow, and pain. I mean, I can honestly say that I can't remember ever being happy. Not even once. And whenever someone came around trying to make me happy, I'd run them off. Because #1, I would think it was only a game they were trying to run on me or something. And #2, I didn't want to be happy. I was so used to being miserable and feeling sorry for myself that I believed that my life was meant to be lived just like that. But thank God for Pat. I couldn't run her off. And Lord knows I've tried. But she just wouldn't let up. And do you want to know something? I'm glad Judge Davis, that she didn't let up or give up on me. In fact, I thank God for bringing her into my life. Because if it wasn't for Pat, I wouldn't be (in mind & spirit) where I am today. Pat has shown me unconditional love & friendship.

Which is something I've never felt from anyone. I would've never have come to know the Lord as I do now if it wasn't for Pat. And I just thank her and love her so much. Through Pat's dedication, perseverance and unconditional love, and teachings, I've come to learn and understand that in Christ I can be happy, in Christ I can and will have a life. And sir, I can honestly tell you that today I am happy. Today, I feel more alive than I've ever felt in my life. I mean, I feel so new. And I can't explain it no other way than to say it is the spirit in me that allows me to be what others see today (a happy man). And I owe it all to Pat. I mean, she actually loved me into Christ.

Pat Howard was Jesus to this man, Brian. These loyal yokefellows bring hope by their willingness to touch the untouchables. Our prisons are full of men and women hungry for the truth, hungry for God. These men and women hunger to be loved, accepted and forgiven in God's sight.

Yet, the laborers are few. "The harvest is plentiful, but the workers are few. Ask the Lord of the harvest, therefore, to send out workers into his harvest field" (Luke 10:2). Pat Howard, Dub Pearson, and many others in prison ministry are doing a great work. They love it, and it is like spiritual food to them.

"My food," said Jesus, "is to do the will of him who sent me and to finish his work. Do you not say, 'Four months more and then the harvest?' I tell you, open your eyes and look at the fields! They are ripe for harvest. Even now the reaper draws his wages, even now he harvests the crop for eternal life, so that the sower and the reaper may be glad together. Thus the saying 'One sows and another reaps' is true. I sent you to reap what you have not worked for. Others have done the hard work, and you have reaped the benefits of their labor."

John 4:34-38

There is a great need for people who are willing to be a witness for the Lord to these inmates – people who will extend the human touch. When Jesus comes in glory, "the King will say to those on his right, 'Come, you who are blessed by my Father; take your inheritance, the kingdom prepared for you since the creation of the world. For I was hungry and you gave me something to eat, I was thirsty and you gave me something to drink, I was a stranger and you invited me in, I needed clothes and you clothed me, I was sick and you looked after me, I was in prison and you came to visit me'" (Matt. 25:34-36). Oh, that true Christians in this country would awaken to see how they can show their love for God and their love for their neighbor by reaching the masses in prison!

Beyond my desire to get this little book into the hands of many inmates, I hope that many people in the free world will be moved to go into the prisons. God bless you and thank you, dear reader, and may He make His love known to you in a very real and intimate way.

The author welcomes your comments and criticisms. You can e-mail him at <u>rickdavis@zenaspublishinghouse.com</u>.

Endnotes

Acknowledgments

1. You can listen to the story of the Man on George Street at www.zenaspublishinghouse.com/georgestreet.MP3.

2. Charles Haddon Spurgeon, "PAUL - His Cloak and His Books," *Metropolitan Tabernacle Pulpit* 9, sermon 542 (1863): 668.

Chapter 1

3. Taken from June 1 reading in *My Utmost for His Highest* by Oswald Chambers, edited by James Reimann, © 1992 by Oswald Chambers Publications Assn., Ltd., and used by permission of Discovery House Publishers, Grand Rapids MI 49501. All rights reserved.

4. The hearing was in December 2006.

5. The letter is real and is still in my possession. I have Brian's permission to use his testimony.

6. T.Y.C. is the Texas Youth Commission, a place where juvenile delinquents are incarcerated.

7. He refers to unauthorized use of a motor vehicle.

8. Alexis de Tocqueville, *Democracy in America*, vol. 1 of *Everyman's Library* (New York: Alfred E. Knopf, 1994), 303.

9. Raspberry, W The Elephant's Tale. (1999, March 5). *Washington Post*, p. A33.

10. See, for example, Smuts, B. No More Wire Mothers, Ever. (2003, February 2). *The New York Times*, p. Sect. 7, p. 19.

Chapter 2

11. In the south, swimming pools are often constructed by the Gunite method, where concrete is pneumatically applied. After the hole for a pool is dug and sculpted and after the iron rebar is installed, Gunite is applied to form the concrete floor, walls, steps and spas of a pool. A Gunite rig mixes dry Portland cement with sand and uses compressed air to shoot the mixture out of a large hose (about the size of a fire hose). A water hose is attached to nozzle of the air hose and the water actually mixes with the cement mix in the air as it is being shot. The concrete mixture sticks to the walls and floor of the pool. It is hot, dirty work. When concrete cures, the reaction is exothermic. That is, it liberates heat as it hardens, and the bottom of the pool under construction gets really hot. The texture of the concrete after it is shot is like the appearance of broken Styrofoam. Men with fresnos, trowels and other tools sculpt it smooth. The

waste material, which is about the consistency of wet sand, falls to the bottom of the pool, where another man, the rebounder, shovels it out from the bottom of the pool over the edge.

12. Freshmen in the Texas Aggie Corps of Cadets are called "fish."

13. Campus Crusade for Christ International is an interdenominational ministry. As the world's largest Christian ministry, Campus Crusade for Christ serves people in one hundred ninety-one countries. It was started by Bill and Vonette Bright as a college ministry at UCLA in 1951.

14. For the second half of the summer, I went to the Far East on a Midshipman's cruise as required by the Navy ROTC contract.

15. I was wrong about the storm. As a result of Hurricane Alicia, Houston suffered billions of dollars in damage. Thousands of glass panes in downtown skyscrapers were shattered by gravel blown off rooftops. In the end, Alicia killed twenty-one people, and was the worst Hurricane to hit Texas since Hurricane Carla in 1961.

Chapter 3

16. Later in life, I had gum surgery to repair a receding gum line. The condition was probably caused by my previous heavy oral tobacco use.

17. In later years, I learned that the teaching that I had through the University about the Bible is considered quite liberal, and often unorthodox. For example, I did

not learn until later that higher criticism is considered controversial, and is rejected by many conservative Christians. Over the years, my confidence in the perfection of the Word has increased rather than decreased.

18. The statute was originally set forth in §42.07 (a)(7), Texas Penal Code.

19. After that, the legislature rewrote the statute and removed the constitutional infirmity.

20. In fairness, the standard for parole revocation is "preponderance of the evidence;" a lower standard than "beyond a reasonable doubt," which is the standard in an ordinary criminal case. It is theoretically possible that the State might be able to prove that a person probably did a crime (in a parole revocation hearing) while it could not prove it beyond a reasonable doubt.

21. Usually, applications for injunction seek to restrain a person from doing something. Although less frequently employed, it is possible to file an application for injunctive relief to require a person to do something; here, to require the mother to turn the boy over that evening.

22. Taken from Feb. 15 reading in *My Utmost for His Highest* by Oswald Chambers, edited by James Reimann, © 1992 by Oswald Chambers Publications Assn., Ltd., and used by permission of Discovery House Publishers, Grand Rapids MI 49501. All rights reserved.

23. Taylor, H (1989). *Hudson Taylor's Spiritual Secret*. Chicago, IL: Moody Press, p. 154.

Chapter 4

24. This message was originally entitled "The Law, Grace, and the Other Side of the Cross" and was also presented to TAX Chapter at the Pack Unit, Navasota, Texas on March 3, 2005, and to the TAX Chapter at the Estelle Unit, Hunstville, Texas on August 31, 2004.

25. Taken from June 1 reading in *My Utmost for His Highest* by Oswald Chambers, edited by James Reimann, © 1992 by Oswald Chambers Publications Assn., Ltd., and used by permission of Discovery House Publishers, Grand Rapids MI 49501. All rights reserved.

26. The Greek word here translated as "faith" is *pistis*. Some translations translate *pistis* as "faithfulness," but in 239 of the 244 New Testament occurrences of this Greek word *pistis*, the KJV renders the word as "faith." On only one occasion does the KJV render the Greek word *pistis* as "fidelity" (a synonym for faithfulness), and that is found in Titus 2:10. The Lord was clearly speaking of soul-saving faith, not faithfulness like a devotion to duty.

27. Taken from Nov. 2 reading in *My Utmost for His Highest* by Oswald Chambers, edited by James Reimann, © 1992 by Oswald Chambers Publications Assn., Ltd., and used by permission of Discovery House Publishers, Grand Rapids MI 49501. All rights reserved.

Chapter 5

28. This message was originally entitled "Marriage: A Holy Institution Given by God."

29. (2004, October 5). Divorce rate no lower among the born-again. *Christian Century.*

30. Lewis, C.S., *The Four Loves* (Orlando, FL: Harcourt Brace Jovanovich, 1960.), p. 114. Used by permission of Harcourt Brace Jovanovich. For the United Kingdom, THE FOUR LOVES by C.S. Lewis copyright © C.S. Lewis Pte. Ltd. 1960, used by permission.

31. Nee, Watchman. *Twelve Baskets Full vol. 4.* (Hong Kong: Hong Kong Church Book Room, 1975.). Note: quote was found in Harrison, N. *His Victorious Indwelling* (Grand Rapids, MI: Zondervan, 1998.) p. 30.

32. Lee, Witness. *Truth Lessons - Level 3 vol. 1.* (Anaheim, CA: Living Stream Ministry, 2001.) p. 22.

Chapter 6

33. Taken from June 1 reading in *My Utmost for His Highest* by Oswald Chambers, edited by James Reimann, © 1992 by Oswald Chambers Publications Assn., Ltd., and used by permission of Discovery House Publishers, Grand Rapids MI 49501. All rights reserved.

34. Nee, Watchman, *What Shall This Man Do?* (Eastbourne, England: Kingsway Publications, 1998.) p. 38. Permission granted by Kingsway Publications, Eastbourne, UK.

Chapter 7

35. "Transformations in the Bible." *Christian Action Magazine* Vol. 2(2003). Retrieved from http://www. christianaction.org.za/articles_ca/2003-2-transformations_bible.htm.

36. John Wesley, Sermon #34 "THE ORIGINAL, NATURE, PROPERTY, AND USE OF THE LAW" (1872).

Chapter 8

37. The Virgin Mary's Hebrew name is "Miriam." Miriam was also the name of Moses' sister who rebelled against Moses' authority in Numbers 12. The name Miriam means "rebel," and these two Miriams may be said to symbolize both the bride of Christ and our sinful rebelliousness. God loves us even though we are ungrateful rebels as were the people in Jabesh Gilead. We need only accept the sacrifice that He provided for us through Jesus Christ to be reconciled to God.

Chapter 9

38. St. Augustine, *Confessions*, ed. Fleming H. Revell (Grand Rapids, MI: Baker Book House, 2005), 34.

39. E.G. Rupp and Benjamin Drewery, eds., *Martin Luther: Documents of Modern History* (New York: St. Martin's Press, 1970), 72-73.

40. Murray, A (1982). *Humility*. New Kensington, PA: Whitaker House. p. 76.

41. Murray, A (1984). *Covenants and blessings*. New Kensington, PA: Whitaker House. p. 143.

Chapter 10

42. Taken from June 1 reading in *My Utmost for His Highest* by Oswald Chambers, edited by James Reimann, © 1992 by Oswald Chambers Publications Assn., Ltd., and used

by permission of Discovery House Publishers, Grand Rapids MI 49501. All rights reserved.

43. The name came from a poem called "Concord Hymn" written by Ralph Waldo Emerson in 1837.

44. Ryan, D. M. (1999, May). The concord fight and a fearless Isaac Davis. *Concord Magazine*, from http://www.concordma.com/magazine/may99/davis.html.

45. Henry, M. (1721). *Commentary on the whole Bible IV (Isaiah to Malachi)*.

46. (2005, November). NOAA reviews record-setting 2005 Atlantic hurricane season. *NOAA News Online*, from http://www.noaanews.noaa.gov/stories2005/s2540.htm.

47. (2005, December). Record Atlantic hurricane season. *World Meteorological Organization*, from http://www.wmo.ch/meteoworld/archive/en/dec2005/hurricane.htm.

48. *Id.*

49. (2004, December). NOAA reports record number of tornadoes in 2004. *NOAA News Online*, from http://www.noaanews.noaa.gov/stories2004/s2359.htm.

50. Berman, A. (2005, December 5). Great sumatra-andaman earthquake of December 2004. *Houston Geological Society*, from http://www.hgs.org/en/art/?708.

51. Walton, M. (2005, May 20). Scientists: Sumatra quake longest ever recorded. *CNN.com*, from http://www.cnn.com/2005/TECH/science/05/19/sumatra.quake/

52. (2005, October 19). New figures put quake toll at more than 79,000. *MSNBC.com*, from http://www.cnn.com/2005/TECH/science/05/19/sumatra.quake/

53. White, M. (2004 December). 30 Worst atrocities of the 20th century. *The Hemoclysm*, from http://users.erols.com/mwhite28/atrox.htm.

54. (2005 November). Masked youths torch bus as Paris rioters set woman afire as violence spreads. *FOXNews.com*, from http://www.foxnews.com/story/0,2933,174533,00.html.

55. (2005 November). French PM calls for 'urgent' reform. *CNN.com*, from http://www.cnn.com/SPECIALS/2005/france.riots/

56. Himmelfard, G. (1994 Fall). A de-moralized society: the British/American experience. *Public Interest*.

57. Retrieved February 13, 2007, from *www.8e6.com* Web site: http://www.8e6home.com/vitalfacts.asp.

58. Gaines, S. (2002/02/28). Why sex still leads the net. *Guardian*.

59. Dyar, J Cyber-porn held responsible for increase in sex addiction; Mental health experts warn of adverse impact on job, family. (2000, January 26). *Washington Times*, p. A2.

60. (2001/01/01). The Leadership survey on pastors and internet pornography. *Leadership*, 22 (1).

61. Means, P. & Means, M. (2000/03). The high-tech snare of the pornographer. *Pastor's Family Bulletin*, 2 (2).

62. *Ibid.*

63. *Maynard v. Hill*, 125 U.S. 190, 211 (1888).

64. *Meyer v. Nebraska*, 262 U.S. 390, 399 (1923).

65. *Skinner v. Oklahoma ex rel. Williamson*, 316 U.S. 535, 541 (1942).

66. Himmelfard, G. (1994 Fall). A de-moralized society: the British/American experience. *Public Interest*.

67. (2004, October 5). Divorce rate no lower among the born-again. *Christian Century*.

68. D. Powell, "Divorce-on-Demand: Forget about Gay Marriage- What About the State of Regular Marriage?," *National Review* 55, no. 20 (2003).

69. Retrieved February 13, 2007, from Bibleinfo.com Web site: http://en.bibleinfo.com/questions/question.html?id=724.

70. The Barna Group, www.barna.org. Barna Update 6/1/2006 Religious Beliefs Vary Widely By Denomination (2001). Accessed 12/06. Used by permission.

71. U. Siemon-Netto, "Poll shows protestant collapse," *United Press International,* June 28, 2001.

72. *Ibid.*

73. *Ibid.*

74. List of states with nuclear weapons. Retrieved February 13, 2007, from www.wikipedia.com Web site: http://en.wikipedia.org/wiki/List_of_states_with_nuclear_weapons.

75. (2005, February 3). Retrieved February 13, 2007, from News - Committee on International Relations Web site: http://internationalrelations.house.gov/archives/109/news021705.htm.

76. Sublette, C. (2002, May 18). http://nuclearweaponarchive.org. Retrieved February 13, 2007, from News - Committee on International Relations Web site: http://nuclearweaponarchive.org/News/Lebedbomb.html.

77. Brennan, P. (2002, Sept. 17). www.NewsMax.com. Retrieved February 13, 2007, from Soviet Nukes Missing. Web site: http://www.newsmax.com/archives/articles/2002/9/17/155150.shtml.

78. After Israel was reborn as a nation in 1948, Weizmann served as the first president of Israel.

79. Balfour, A. (1917, November 2). http://www.fordham.edu/halsall/mod/modsbook.html. Retrieved February 13, 2007, from Modern history sourcebook: the balfour declaration Web site: http://www.fordham.edu/halsall/mod/balfour.html.

80. McCrackan, W. D. (1922). *The New Palestine*. Boston, MA: p. 93.

81. Reagan, D. Hurricane Katrina. *Lamplighter*, Retrieved February 13, 2007, from http://www.lamblion. com/articles/prophecy/signs/Signs-10.php.

82. *Id.*

83. *Id.*

84. *Id.*

85. (2005, November 3). Retrieved February 14, 2007, from *CNN.com*. Web site: http://www.cnn.com/2005/ US/11/15/tuesday/index.html

86. The Greek word that is translated "tempest" here is *seismos*. The NIV translates the word "a great storm." Everywhere else the word seismos appears in the New Testament, however, it is translated "earthquake."

Chapter 11

87. Packer, J.I., *Knowing God* (Downers Grove, IL: InterVaristy Press, 1973), 141.

88. Fabelo, T., *Justice Reinvestment: A Framework to Improve Effectiveness of Justice Policies in Texas* (presented to the 80th Texas Legislature, 2007).

Book Ordering Information

ζηναν

Zenas Publishing House
P.O. Box 1206
Bryan, Texas 77806

www.zenaspublishinghouse.com

Want to get a copy of
The Prison Sermons for a friend?
You can order the book through:
www.amazon.com,
www.barnesandnobles.com,
www.booksamillion.com,
www.borders.com,
www.target.com
or any other major bookseller.

****

But for FASTEST delivery, order directly from our printer 24/7 by calling 1-866-909-BOOK (2665) or by visiting www.xulonpress.com/bookstore.php and the book will be shipped straight from the printer to you.

****

SHIPPING & HANDLING REBATE for copies of *The Prison Sermons* that you order for a Texas prison inmate. If you order a copy of the book for a Texas inmate –or– if you order a bulk purchase of books for a Chaplaincy in a Texas prison, Zenas Publishing House will rebate you the actual cost you pay for Shipping and Handling (up to 25% of the purchase price). Simply contact us at the e-mail address shown below.

****

E-mail us at info@zenaspublishinghouse.com with any other questions you may have.

Printed in the United States
91339LV00005B/38/A

9 781602 660564